FROM

WALKING TOURS

Spain's
Favorite Cities

Herbert Bailey Livesey

MACMILLAN • USA

ABOUT THE AUTHOR

Herbert Bailey Livesey became a freelance writer following a career in higher education, including Director of Admissions at New York University. He has written articles for such magazines as Travel & Leisure; 5 of his published books concern travel in Canada, Iberia, and the United States. He and his wife Joanne own a house in rural Spain, but live most of the year in the Hudson River Valley.

MACMILLAN TRAVEL

A Simon & Schuster Macmillan Company
1633 Broadway
New York, NY 10019

Copyright © 1995 by Simon & Schuster, Inc.

ISBN 0-02-860473-3
ISSN 1082-1481

Editor: Charlotte Allstrom
Map Editor: Douglas Stallings
Digital cartography by Ortelius Design
Design by Amy Peppler Adams—designLab, Seattle

SPECIAL SALES

Bulk purchases (10+ copies) of Frommer's Travel Guides are available to corporations at special discounts. The Special Sales Department can produce custom editions to be used as premiums and/or for sales promotion to suit individual needs. Existing editions can be produced with custom cover imprints such as corporate logos. For more information write to: Special Sales, Macmillan, 1633 Broadway, New York, NY 10019.

Manufactured in the United States of America

CONTENTS

LIST OF MAPS

An Invitation to the Reader

In researching this book, I have come across many wonderful sights, cafés, and restaurants, the best of which I have included here. I am sure that many of you will also discover appealing places as you explore Spain. Please don't keep them to yourself. Share your experiences, especially if you want to bring to my attention information that has changed since this book was researched. You can address your letters to:

Herbert Bailey Livesey
Frommer's Walking Tours: Spain's Favorite Cities
Macmillan Travel
1633 Broadway
New York, NY 10019

An Additional Note

Please be advised that travel information is subject to change at any time. The author, editors, and publisher cannot be held responsible for the experiences of readers while traveling. Your safety is important to us, however, so we encourage you to stay alert and be aware of your surroundings. Keep a close eye on cameras, purses, and wallets, all favorite targets of thieves and pickpockets.

Introducing Spain's Favorite Cities

Ask 10 Spaniards the same question and get 11 answers. That contrariness is hardly surprising in a country comprising dozens of principalities and fervently proclaimed mininations, with three official languages and twice as many dialects. The world's perception of Spain might be of olive groves, eternal sun, endless beaches, ruined castles, and fiery dancers who shatter the air with the drilling of heels and clapping of hands. Those are all gratifyingly there, as exhilarating as ever. Other Spains, though, are green, cool valleys buffeted by Atlantic storms, summer snow on mountains an hour from the Mediterranean, and citizens who think nothing of going to the office directly from their last nightclub.

So it is with her cities, as diverse and diverting a group as that found in any country in Europe. Madrid, not much older than Boston or Montreal, was long adjudged to be one of the most repressed and provincial capitals anywhere. Yet it is the treasury of a former empire and currently nurtures art movements and the attendant nightlife that keeps "swinging Madrid" up past dawn. By contrast, Phoenician and Greek traders probably touched down at Barcelona before the Romans became established. At its core is an intact medieval city atop a town built by Augustus. Picasso, Miró, and a visionary architect by the apt name of Gaudí gave Barcelona much of its visual verve, a tradition continued by contemporary artists and designers who challenge the best of Paris and Milan. The conquering tribal groups of Arabs and Berbers (collectively known as the Moors) stayed in Iberia for almost 800 years, clinging the longest to their provinces in southern Spain. Granada still has a hilltop fantasy of palaces, forts, and gardens—the last magnificent remains of their occupation. Pride of place in Córdoba is a mosque that covers 6 acres with a single roof. Seville, a river city with access to a familiar sea and an unknown ocean, was a conduit to the New World, much of whose passing riches stuck to Sevillano fingers. And Salamanca with its prestigious university was the rivaled seat of learning in the Middle Ages, marked by a group of extraordinary edifices representing the highest levels of architectural achievement during the Renaissance.

All six cities are explored by the following walking itineraries. Apart from a few short stretches, they consist of flat terrain or easily negotiated slopes. These suggested routes are not intended to be comprehensive, but they include most of the major attractions in each city as well as detours to secret nooks and hidden cul-de-sacs that often constitute the highlights of a visit. If these cities whet your appetite, Spain offers many other possibilities for walking tours, including: Santiago de Compostela, Burgos, Mérida, Toledo, and Caceres.

BARCELONA

Approached from the sea, Barcelona looks as if it is cradled in a great cupped hand—a left hand, to be precise. At the wrist edge of the palm is the Mediterranean. To the west of the harbor is a thumb pad of hill called Montjuïc, and at the back are the curled fingers of a massif dominated by the peak of Tibidabo. At the center of the palm is the broad Plaça de Catalunya where several major arteries intersect, and trailing off the Plaça down to the harbor is the lifeline known as La Rambla, a boulevard arched over with a double row of trees. Apart from church steeples and a few unfortunate attempts at skyscrapers, the city's buildings rarely exceed eight stories in height, preserving the visual harmony of the grid plan of the Eixample. That district fills the gentle slope between the old city at the water's edge and the

Barcelona: The Tours at a Glance

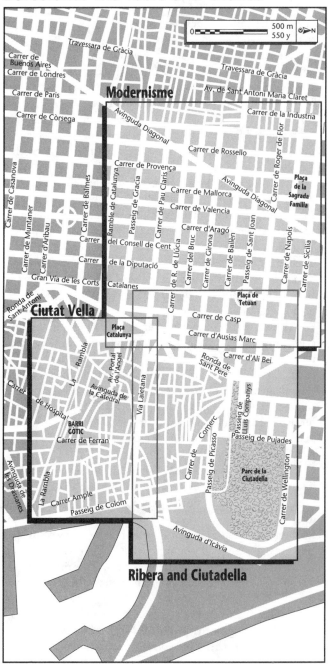

Travessara de Gràcia

Carrer de Buenos Aires

Carrer de Londres

Carrer de Paris

Modernisme

Travessara de Gràcia

Av. de Sant Antoni Maria Claret

Carrer de Còrsega

Carrer de la Industria

Avinguda Diagonal

Carrer de Rossello

Carrer de Roger de Flor

Carrer de Casanova

Carrer de Muntaner

Carrer d'Aribau

Carrer de Bàlmes

Ramble de Catalunya

Passeig de Gracia

Carrer de Pau Claris

Carrer de Provença

Carrer de Mallorca

Avinguda Diagonal

Plaça de la Sagrada Familia

Carrer de Valencia

Carrer

Carrer d'Aragó

Carrer

del Consell de Cent

Carrer de R. de Llúcia

Carrer del Bruc

Carrer de Girona

Carrer de Bailén

Passeig de Sant Joan

Carrer de Napols

Carrer de Sicilia

de la Diputació

Gran Vía de les Corts

Catalanes

Plaça de Tetuan

Ronda de Sant Antoni

Ciutat Vella

Plaça Catalunya

Carrer de Casp

Carrer d'Ausias Marc

Carrer d'Ali Bei

La Rambla

Carrer de Hospital

La Rambla

Av. Portal de l'Angel

Avinguda de la Catedral

BARRI GÒTIC

Carrer de Ferran

Via Laietana

Ronda de Sant Pere

Carrer de Comerc

Passeig de Picasso

Passeig de Lluis Companys

Passeig de Pujades

Parc de la Ciutadella

Carrer de Wellington

Avinguda de les Drassanes

La Rambla

Carrer Ample

Passeig de Colom

Avinguda d'Icària

Ribera and Ciutadella

0   500 m
     550 y
N

incorporated former suburbs that ease up to the mountain range to the north.

Stone Age tribes populated this shore in what is now the northeast corner of Spain long before the Phoenicians and Greeks stopped by to set up trading posts in the 6th century B.C. They were still there when the Romans arrived in the vicinity of Barcelona about 300 years later to engage the Carthaginians in the first of the Punic Wars. Nothing remains of the Laietani, as the Romans called them, and precious little more of the Phoenicians and Greeks.

Evidence of the long Roman rule is substantial, however, including much of the defensive wall they built around their colony, the surviving columns of a great temple, and the remnants of a village that lie beneath the palaces of medieval counts. This does not imply that the Romans invested unusual amounts of effort and treasure in the colony. The cities of Tarragona (about 40 miles to the south) and Mérida (near Portugal) were far more important. Barcelona's harbor was poor and there were no important mineral deposits.

Growth was slow, then, even after the settlement was officially named Barcino shortly before the birth of Christ. By then, the defensive walls were under construction, enclosing a rectangular area of about 25 acres, with the forum and market at the central intersection of the two main streets. The entrances were confined to four city gates, one in each wall. By the third century A.D., the walls had been strengthened and augmented with as many as 78 towers. Not long after, Constantine made Christianity the official religion of his realm.

The decline of the Roman Empire had already begun, but it was another century until the fierce Germanic tribes that had been rampaging across Europe poured over the Pyrenees. Vandals, Suevians, and Alani swept through Catalunya and on into southern and western Iberia. They were soon followed by the Visigoths, thousands of whom stayed in Barcino. They went on to defeat the tribes that had preceded them. Once the Visigoths were in full control (by A.D. 476), the Romans had withdrawn completely from the peninsula.

In historical terms, the Visigothic suzerainty was short-lived. Arab tribes living in the deserts of North Africa were casting covetous eyes on fertile Iberia and its apparent abundance of gushing water. They thundered across the Straits of Gibraltar in

A.D. 711 and swept across most of the peninsula, including Catalunya, in less than 10 years.

The Arabs ("Moors" is a loose and essentially inaccurate term) pushed across into France but were repelled by the Franks, first under Charlemagne and then by his son, Louis the Pious. Barcelona was free of Arab rule after A.D. 801, except for a brief period in the late 10th century. But the period of Moorish dominion was essentially past, and as they were forced southward, they were replaced by independent kingdoms and fiefdoms—the beginning of feudalism and the Dark Ages.

The counts of Barcelona expanded what was known as the Spanish march into southern France, and, as part of the Aragonese-Catalan alliance, established colonies and trading centers in Valencia, Sardinia, Sicily, and Greece. After the Arabs were expelled from their last stronghold in Granada in 1492, the Catholic monarchs, Isabel and Fernando, set about consolidating their hold on the various kingdoms and separatist-minded territories. Catalunya posed a problem for every Spanish central government over the next five centuries. Attempts to extend Spanish rule over the Catalans never completely succeeded, although successive kings repeatedly fought with the rebels. Walls were erected around Barcelona, encompassing a much larger area than that of the Romans. They were intended both to contain the Barcelonese and to protect them. In the early 18th century, Felipe V ordered construction of an immense fortress, the Ciutadella (Citadel), symbol of the hated centralist monarchs of Madrid.

The Citadel and its walls were torn down in the mid-19th century. This took more than 10 years, during which time, plans were made to develop the essentially empty territory between the old city and the villages to the north and west. What finally emerged was a regular gridwork of streets called the Eixample (or Extension), slashed by a few diagonal feeder boulevards. This design had a Parisian flavor, which wasn't surprising, since it had been inspired (at least in part) by the then-current restructuring of the City of Light. The Eixample became the primary home of the architectural and design movement known as *modernisme,* a peculiarly Catalan version of art nouveau.

Barcelona led Spain into the Industrial Revolution. It proclaimed that achievement in 1888 by staging a Universal Exposition—an event that enabled it once again to carry out some ambitious urban planning. Another exposition, in 1929, led to further enhancement of the city's infrastructure. Finally, the 1992 Summer Olympics prompted an upgrading of the airport, the metro system, and a network of roads. More than 25 miles of previously inaccessible beaches were opened to the public, and a satellite city was built on the former site of abandoned warehouses and railroad switching yards.

Today, Barcelona is more appealing than ever, a place where people are comfortable with their heritage and are seeking full recognition of its status as the most European of Spanish cities.

MADRID

"A city in the making," was C. Gasquoine Hartley's description of Madrid in a 1921 guidebook. This was a mild pronouncement, for the rest of the Continent generally viewed Madrid as dully provincial, even backward, when measured against such cities as Paris, Rome, and London. There was truth in Hartley's characterization, but now it has taken on a positive spin, suggesting a place that is restless, on the make, rather than simply unfinished.

Start with a wide-angle view of the city. Madrid sprawls at the center of a vast plateau called the *Meseta*. Since nearly unbroken mountain chains back the four shores of the rectangular Iberian peninsula and the middle consists of this high tableland, Spain has been broad-brushed topographically as an empty picture frame. The fact is that Madrid is far from being a mere urban interruption on a windswept plain. To the west and north are the substantial Sierras de Gredos and Guadarrama. To the east is the Rio Jarama, which merges in the south with the Rio Tajo on its long journey west to Lisbon and the Atlantic. Both rivers originate in the Guadarrama.

Those features are obvious from a height of 10,000 feet. Move closer and you can observe treeless tawny pastures inside that ring of mountains and rivers, sectioned by roads that radiate from the capital. Patches of cultivated green accumulate as irrigation systems proliferate nearer the city, soon giving way to suburban housing tracts and the usual dross of tank farms and junkyards. If it were possible to hover above the city itself, the most evident feature would be the Paseo de Castellana, an unusually broad boulevard that runs north–south with streams of vehicles at all hours. A parallel new beltway recently completed

Madrid: The Tours at a Glance

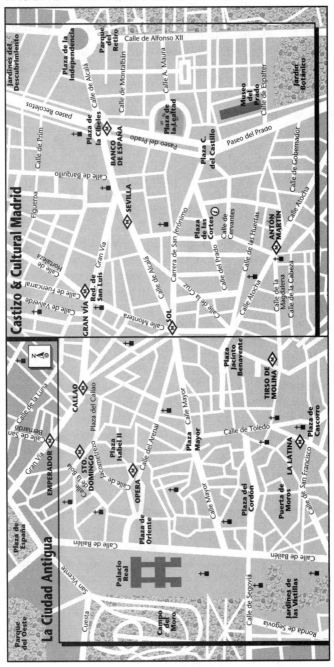

along the eastern edge of the city has succeeded in diverting a lot of traffic from the center, although it might not seem that way during one of the four daily rush hours. The upper reaches of the Paseo are lined with government buildings and expensive hotels and bristle with glass office towers that get taller as they spread northward, only to peter out around the Chamartín railroad station. Most of the midrisers (none qualify as skyscrapers) are of recent construction. Although a few of them are oddly designed, none makes a significant contribution to the architectural esthetic canon. This modern extension city was devastated farmland at the end of the 1936–39 Civil War. Although this part of town is where businesspeople are likely to spend their working hours, and it has most of the prominent expense-account hotels, restaurants, and nightclubs, it has little charm.

The leisure and enlightenment sought by most visitors are found primarily along or below the Calle de Alcalá, an avenue that cuts across the city from east to west. Alcalá eventually runs into the Puerta del Sol, a knot of 10 converging streets. Two of those, the Calles Arenal and Mayor, continue out the other side and roll down to the banks of Manzanares, a torpid stream accorded undeserved river status. Within a block or two of that ganglia of arteries are the Prado Museum, the new Thyssen-Bornemisza Museum, and the Royal Palace, the three must-see cultural sights. To the south and southwest of the Puerta del Sol lie the oldest *barrios*. They have a few architectural survivors from the 15th and 16th centuries, but most of the houses and commercial structures are less than 200 years old. These tangled narrow streets shelter hundreds of the taverns, bars, restaurants, and intimate music and dance clubs that keep Madrileños up all night.

That last observation is literal. No city in Europe surpasses Madrid in the numbers of hours it devotes each day to diversion. Restaurants open at 1:30pm for lunch but rarely start filling up before 2:30. The meal ends at 4 or even 5pm. Then Madrileños return to school or work and put in another three or four hours before spilling out into the streets once again. They join family or friends and start walking. This is the *paseo,* an unofficial Spanish ritual that takes place every night throughout the year, in large cities as well as in rural hamlets comprising barely four blocks. Flirting and gossiping and promenading leads to thirst, so frequent stops are made at the bars on nearly every corner. Adults consume squat little tumblers of *tinto* (red wine) or glasses of beer, and their children drink Cokes or other *refrescos*. Most of these bars or *mesónes* serve a communal function, where families are welcome. Since it is too early for dinner, they order *tapas*—tasty little snacks that Madrileños and other Spaniards eat before the main meal, which comes later. Often, stopping for drinks becomes a *tapas* crawl, sampling house specialities at several bars, a practice that is known as *tapeo*. Around 9 or 9:30pm, families return home to prepare their evening meal or nap or make arrangements to meet later. Dinner is usually served around 10:30pm, although it isn't unusual for upper-class Madrileños to meet for drinks then and go on to their chosen restaurants at midnight.

That leaves some time to spare, since the discos and night-clubs don't swing into action until much later. The interlude may be filled with drinks at a "bar of the night," one that serves cocktails and highballs but little or no food. By 2 or 3am, it's time to move on to one of the larger discos or *multispacios*, which may feature two or more dance floors and several bars with laser shows and live bands, supplemented by in-house restaurants, pool tables, and even bowling lanes. They close at 4 or 5am, but not to worry. Still other clubs don't open until then and remain open until 9 or 10am.

Somehow, buses and trains meet their schedules, banks change money, and shops and offices carry on their normal work. No one has quite figured out how this can be, given the Madrileño social schedule. But at least one can understand why so many Madrileños appear to need sleep.

Madrid isn't youthful only in its pursuit of pleasure or in the fact that children keep much the same hours as their parents. By European standards, it is a young city; it was only 430 years ago that Felipe II declared Madrid the capital. At the time, Madrid was little more than an isolated farm village beside an unreliable stream. To understand the impact of Felipe II's decision, suppose that the U.S. Congress decided to move the capital to the approximate center of the continental United States. That would be Lebanon, Kansas (population 364). Then substitute the likely reactions of New York, Chicago, and Los Angeles for those of Barcelona, Valencia, and Seville.

Felipe II was unfazed by the predictable uproar from the perimeter of his domain. He started building himself a center for his court, commencing with a suitable Plaza Mayor. The second in the Hapsburg line to rule Spain, he and his successors (who were followed by the Bourbons at the start of the 18th century) are responsible for the layout of the city as it appears today and for most of the monuments and notable buildings that line its avenues. The Hapsburgs can claim Felipe's Plaza Mayor, the cluster of governmental buildings at the Plaza de la Villa, the art-filled Monasterio de las Descalzas Reales, and the Catedral de San Isidro, among others. The Bourbon line, which includes the current king, Juan Carlos, held sway during construction of the huge Royal Palace and the Prado Museum, the city's two most impressive repositories.

Mythmakers and fabulists still tend to overlook Madrid, but faint praise is no longer its lot. The city has finally come of age.

GRANADA

No Spanish city enjoys a more arresting physical setting. Granada clambers over and folds around three sharply defined foothills that thrust out into a wide fertile plain called the *vega*. Its backdrop is the magisterial curtain wall of the Sierra Nevada, whose sawtooth peaks are dusted with snow well past spring, even this close to Saharan Africa. The Costa del Sol, along the southern rim of Iberia, is only 50 miles away, which makes it possible at certain times of the year to ski in the morning in the Sierra Nevada and to windsurf in the Mediterranean in the afternoon.

While modern and newly prosperous Granada pushes its suburban silt out across quilted farmlands and into orchards of citrus and olive trees, the interest of most visitors is concentrated on those three hills—Albaicín, Sacramonte, and Alhambra. The last of these is the reason to make this journey. It is a wedge of rock that plows into the city below like the prow of a supertanker. High above, the perimeter of its flattened crest bristles with ramparts and watchtowers that can be seen many miles away. Within those battlements is a complex of palaces, citadels, and gardens that surpasses, in both artistry and historical import, any comparable destination in Europe.

Looking down from above, that concentration of structures, enclosed by unbroken but uneven walls, has the shape of an extended finger pointing at the *vega*. At its western tip are the towers of an Arab alcazar that once protected the site. At the first joint of the finger is a palace built by Carlos V, whose grand-parents (Isabel and Fernando) wrested the city from the Arabs in 1492. Next to it is the entrance to the older, less imposing, palace of the Moors. These structures give way to terraced gardens below a 15th-century monastery that is now one of the most esteemed units of the nationwide **parador** chain of more than 80 state-owned inns. Beyond the parador, connected to the eastern end of the Alhambra (as a tail is to a temple cat) is the Generalife, the elevated residence of the emirs who retired there during the summer to enjoy the cooling breezes that rolled down from the mountains and to feel the mists of a multitude of fountains on their faces.

Little wonder that the loss of Spain is said to be lamented even today in prayers in Middle Eastern mosques. When the last Arab ruler conceded victory to the army of the Catholic kings in 1492, he was surrendering the last major emirate on the peninsula. There is a point on the road south to Motril now called *El Ultimo Suspiro de Moro* (The Last Sigh of the Moor). It was more than a sigh, according to most stories. Boabdil stopped there to turn and take a last look at his beloved city, his eyes filling with tears over his great loss. His mother Axia, who was riding beside him, was not the nurturing sort. In words that vary, depending on the translation, she sniffed, "My son, you weep like a woman for the loss of what you could not defend as a man."

Perhaps that scorn was bracing, for although the fall of Granada in 1492 is considered the end of the Moorish presence in Spain, Boabdil went on to lead a series of rebellions from mountain redoubts. For the record, the last stand of the dwindling Moorish resistance was in 1569, in Frigliana—a village only 8 miles from the sea. When they saw that their cause was hopeless in the face of superior Spanish forces, the defiant defenders threw themselves from a cliff to avoid capture.

Granada owes much to the Moors, even its name, which evolved from the Arab word *Karnattah*. This word has nothing to do with the pomegranate, which is *granada* in Spanish. Granada wasn't always the cynosure it had become by 1246, when it was made the capital of the shrinking Moorish territory in Iberia. Until then, it had been something of a backwater in the long shadow cast by the jewel of the empire, Córdoba. When that city fell to Fernando II in 1236, its aristocracy and the cream of its mercantile and artisan classes migrated to the last impor-tant Moorish city in Spain. With that injection of talent, Granada flourished for almost three centuries.

Rulers of first the Almoravid and then the Nasrid Moorish dynasties had the leisure and funds to build scores of mosques and palaces. Most of these are gone now, victims of the royal habit of razing the monuments of their predecessors. That rarity is what makes the Alhambra so remarkable, an achievement whose magical exuberance is comparable with Angkor Wat, the Parthenon, and Chichén Itzá.

The city below the Alhambra is of only fleeting interest, pleasant enough for a meal or two, a *tapas* crawl, an amble through the Gothic-Renaissance cathedral, and a look at the Royal Chapel, where Isabel and Fernando are interred. But the Alhambra deserves at least two contemplative visits, one to ob-tain an overview, and a second to return to its most compelling chambers and patios, perhaps during the limited evening visit-ing hours. If a night can be spent at the popular Parador de San Francisco—an inn in a converted 16th-century monastery on the grounds—so much the better. But make a reservation as far in advance as possible (at least six months). The Alhambra is worth it.

CÓRDOBA

The ancient quarter of Córdoba comes as close to what most of us imagine as stereotypical Spain as any place in Andalucia. Its meandering, cobblestoned streets are lined with whitewashed houses with roofs of semicircular terracotta tiles. Shuttered win-dows are protected by black metal grilles with pots of geraniums crowding their sills, and iron gates open onto inner courtyards dense with ferns and citrus trees, festoons of flowering vines and garden plots, and additional pots of roses, dahlias, and mums of a dozen hues. At night, unseen women are heard singing over the clatter of dishes, and eruptions of castanets shatter the evening shadows.

If possible, approach the old town from the south. The edge of the medieval quarter touches the north bank of a bend in the Guadalquivir ("Great River" in the original Arabic). It is stitched to the modern city on the south shore by a bridge whose foun-dations were laid by the Romans. In their time, and well into the reign of the Moors, the river was navigable all the way past

Seville to the Atlantic. Now, it is so silted that trees grow out in the middle of the stream and cows graze under the arches of the bridge. To the left of the bridge, as seen from the south bank, is a working waterwheel of Arab origin, and rearing up behind bridge and wheel are the tawny outer walls of the Great Mosque, one of Islam's most profoundly affecting monuments.

When the Romans arrived, two centuries before Christ, they found a thriving Iberian community here. By 152 B.C., they had made it the capital of their colony of Baetica. Córdoba's fortunes ebbed and flowed under the Romans, as when it chose the wrong side in a battle for control of Rome in 42 B.C. and Julius Caesar punished the city. Subsequent emperors were more generous than he, and the city grew still more prosperous as the administrative center of all Iberia, which was allowed to become an integral part of Rome, not simply a colony.

Prominent Roman statesmen and thinkers were born here, including the poet and orator Seneca the Elder (55 B.C.–A.D. 39) and his son and grandson, advisers to Caesar and as influential as he in the currents of the Empire. By the 5th century, however, the Visigoths had swept across the peninsula, dislodging the Romans and making Christianity the state religion. They established their capital at Toledo, well to the north, and so Córdoba lost its prominence as well as its wealth and influence. Córdoba's festering resentment of its diminished status eventually worked against the Visigoths. Córdoba's large Jewish community, in particular, suffered discrimination under the Visigoths, and they awaited a chance to free themselves. After the lightning invasion of the Moors in A.D. 711, disgruntled Cordobeses functioned as a fifth column, undermining the Visigoths on behalf of their new masters. They were rewarded with a measure of tolerance and freedom that permitted them to attain positions of influence. From around 750 until the end of the 10th century, Córdoba enjoyed a lengthy renaissance as the capital of Moorish Iberia, the riches of the Islamic world overflowing its coffers.

Jewish philosophers and Arab scholars walked these streets in a communal harmony that would be all but inconceivable today. By the time Córdoba reached its highest point in the 10th century, it had a vigorous population of perhaps 1 million inhabitants, according to some estimates. That made it one of the largest metropolitan areas in Europe, three times the size of today's city. It is believed there were more than 3,000 mosques, and Córdoba was the western anchor of an Islamic empire that reached all the way to Damascus.

Internecine conflicts arose between competing Moorish dynasties, and there were revolts by the fierce Berbers, valued for their capabilities in war but repressed by the ruling elites. These conflicts made Córdoba vulnerable to the glacial but relentless Christian Reconquest that was approaching from the west and north; finally, in 1236, the city fell to the Catholic king, Fernando III. The richest merchants and artisans, as well as the aristocracy, fled to Granada, the last large Moorish holding in Spain.

Drained of talent and treasure, Córdoba once again slid into mediocrity, becoming just another drab provincial capital. Most of the splendid Moorish mosques and palaces were razed or allowed to deteriorate. Commercial interests migrated to Seville, which had more ready access to Mediterranean sea lanes. Apart from a brief resurgence in the late 15th century, when Isabel and Fernando made it their command post for the assault on Granada, Córdoba never again recovered its former glories.

Modern Córdoba still cannot compare with Seville, Barcelona, or Madrid. However, the city is energetic and forward-looking, with enough industry to support most of its burgeoning population (about 73,000 in 1920, but now about 300,000). Little on the south side of the river and the area surrounding the Great Mosque and the adjacent *barrio* (known as the Judería) will probably interest most tourists. However, there is enough to see and do in that compact quarter to engage even a casual visitor for a long weekend.

SEVILLE

This is the most Spanish of cities, as has often been observed. Smeared with symbols assigned to it by others, a superficial crust concealing deeper layers of the national psyche, it is remarkable how lightly Seville bears its burden. Unlike visitors to Madrid or even Barcelona, visitors arrive in Seville with certain expectations of what they will find. These derive from nearly forgotten films and images from travel brochures and bullfight posters: Castles in Spain. Blood and Sand. Gypsies and Flamenco. Red carnations and Suits of Light. White stucco houses draped in jasmine with orange tile roofs. Castanets and guitars sounding on puffs of sultry night air. Cobblestoned streets echoing with hoofbeats and carriage wheels.

Seville delivers. It has all those things and more. Its people and their actions, today and yesterday, reflect elements of a national character. Not *the* national character, for the several semi-nations and ancient kingdoms that comprise Spain are too disparate for such a generalization. But Seville is the de facto capital of southern Spain—the region known as Andalucia— and as such, it is the inescapable repository of long-held ethnic tendencies and cultural assumptions.

Andalucians always live in the present, it is said, because of the multitude of events that clog the yearly calendar: the fiestas, festivals, celebrations, and tributes that routinely take precedence over one's usual work.

Even in the intervals between scheduled happenings, the importance of the moment—*this* moment—prevails. Yesterday is gone and tomorrow is unknown, so fretting about them is wasted energy. Andalucians are unlikely to spend much time reading since newspapers focus on what has already occurred. So people get their real news from television, assuming it is *en vivo,* live, right now. Or, more often, news is imparted by friends, however distorted from reality it might be. That is why friends and family always contrive to be together. Bars in Seville have less to do with the consumption of alcohol than with the gathering of the clans—toddlers to oldsters. Bars are places where people share their triumphs and calamities, consolidate alliances, deplore and venerate. For this reason there is hardly a block in the city that doesn't have at least one or two taverns, filled with patrons from morning coffee to brandy nightcap.

Incongruities are epidemic. Those eternally packed bars and cafés and the stylish dress and carefree demeanor of the citizenry imply prosperity. For many, the impression is accurate, especially in contrast to the dark decades of the Franco regime. But the unemployment rate for Andalucía is acknowledged to be an intractable 25%, which results in significant street crime and homelessness (comparable to the big cities of America). Sevillano pride is expressed in the often spoken belief, "Everyone a nobleman." Yet class distinctions simmer and rankle here as nowhere else in Spain. The titled and/or monied aristocracy keeps a low profile in these days of democracy, but the gap between them and their employees remains unbridgeable. And if any part of Spain is guilty of that hoary *mañana* canard, it is Seville, if only because of the frequent timeouts for civic partying. There is little that can't be dealt with at a later time. That is why the rest of the country was skeptical when Seville said it could mount a world's fair in record time and with Teutonic efficiency. Yet Expo '92, the last of its kind in this century, was an estimable success; Seville benefited from a much-enhanced, up-to-the-minute transportation network of new bridges, high-speed rail service, and a legitimate international airport. Seville arrived at the edge of the 21st century without spending much time in the 20th.

Pragmatism is not a frequent Andalucian trait, but it exists nonetheless. Seville has capitulated with unseemly haste to every determined force that sailed up the Guadalquivir, from Romans to Visigoths to Moors to Catholic kings. The most recent example was the arrival in July 1936 of a vanguard of the Falangist rebellion in the person of General Quiepo de Llano. He drove into the city on July 18th with only a handful of officers. Through bluff and bravado, including a series of bombastic radio addresses, he gained the allegiance of the local garrisons and captured the city (the fourth largest in Spain) just three days later.

One result of Seville's reluctance to take up arms is that it has largely escaped armed hostilities, although there have been a few notable natural diasters and some boneheaded decisions made by some of its rulers. The Moors, who stormed across the straits of Gibraltar in 711, stayed in Seville until they were beaten by the army of Fernando III in 1236. They had built palaces and mosques that might have been as breathtakingly memorable as those that survive in Granada and Córdoba. We will never know, for the victorious Christians leveled the Moorish Alcazar and erected their own palace at the same site; when the archbishops grew dissatisfied with using a converted mosque as their cathedral, they tore it down in the 15th century to build an unmistakably Christian cathedral. At least they kept fragments of the old structures, including a watchtower beside the Guadalquivir River, some palace ramparts that also served as aqueducts, and, most notably, a minaret that is now the belltower of the cathedral.

The hubris that fueled these acts was reinforced by the discovery and exploitation of the mineral and agricultural wealth of Spain's colonial empire across the ocean. Seville, which offered a protected harbor only 80 miles from the Atlantic, became the primary port for the treasure galleons that returned with spoils from the Aztec and Inca nations. The resulting Golden Age was brief in historic terms but long in memory. Murillo and Velázquez were born and worked here. Romantic tales of the city with spiritual ties to Africa and the Middle East inspired composers and such authors as the perambulating Cervantes, while the golden lifeline to a new world of uncounted riches underwrote military campaigns that brought much of Europe under the sway of the Spanish kings.

Seville was a predominant city during much of that time, while Madrid was still taking shape as the artificial capital of a newly unified Spain. When the river filled with silt, merchant ships started to dock at Cádiz, and commerce dried up. Seville (as well as Andalucía) withered into an impoverished land controlled by a small oligarchy of landowners and aristocrats. One consolation, however, was that northern Europeans found its poverty picturesque and its Arabesques exotic. They came expecting drama and a little safe danger, enjoying the sun and the ruins, while leaving pocket change along the way and clucking at what they perceived to be Andalucian sloth and slovenliness.

This is still the case. More than 60 million foreign visitors arrive in Spain every year, exceeding the country's total population. A sizable number pass through Seville, leaving a lot more than change. Romance still exists, and intimacy, and an inalienable zest for life. They just cost more.

SALAMANCA

Ideally, Salamanca should be approached from the south bank of the River Tormes via the old Roman bridge. There isn't much on the south side, while the city itself is as poised, tranquil, and inviting as any on the vast central tableland known as the *Meseta*. Whereas in southern Spain buildings are inclined to be slathered with plaster, here the color of building materials reflects the color of the city. For example, the native stone of Salamanca is sandstone; it soaks up the bright light of midday, taking on a honey glow while turning the slanting rays of dusk into an all-over rosy blush.

Those shifts in tone lend a pleasing unity to the spires and towers of Salamanca, which can be seen to great advantage from the sturdy Roman span. The rush of the river and the rustle of bordering trees serve to dampen the flow of traffic behind and to either side, on a beltway and two bridges intended to serve modern needs. This bridge, though, is just wide enough for pedestrians; Salamanca tolerates motor vehicles only grudgingly. At the end of the bridge is a legless stone bull on a pedestal; although eroded over time, he still projects a certain dignity. Predating the arrival of Hannibal (in 217 B.C.) by centuries, he was presumably a deity of the Celtiberians who dug the foundations of Salamanca. The statue lay at the bottom of the river for many centuries, cast aside, perhaps, by the conquerors, who had their own gods.

As important as the harmonizing color of the city beyond the bull are the uses to which the sandstone has been put. Salamanca's years of glory lasted from the 13th through 17th centuries, when it was home to one of Europe's oldest and most vigorous universities. Gothic and Renaissance architectural styles prevail, flowering especially in the sumptuous Plateresque mode. Sandstone is an ideal material for that demandingly intricate technique, for not only is it highly malleable when first quarried, but also it has the property of hardening with age. Thus, the work of Salamanca's gifted stonecarvers has been preserved. Despite the depredations of warring Romans, Arabs, English, and French, the city flourishes (along with Barcelona and Granada's Alhambra) as one of Spain's greatest architectural legacies.

Also of interest is the fact that education and religion have coexisted uneasily here since the founding of the university in 1215. With the patronage of several enlightened monarchs, Salamanca acquired a reputation as one of the finest universities in the Western world along with the Sorbonne, Bologna, and Oxford. Thus, it attracted an outstanding faculty, who in turn attracted ever-increasing enrollments; this inspired aristocratic families to build noble mansions, terraces, churches, cathedrals, monasteries, and classroom buildings.

Columbus sought the support of university scientists for his theories and got it, easing his task of fund-raising. The university faculty is credited with developing the concept of international law, and it inspired the establishment of the early centers of learning in the New World.

At the time of the Inquisition, the university was extremely well respected. It had survived repeated invasions and the violent vendettas of blue-blooded familes who formed armed groups known as *bandos*. But then the university began to lose its openness toward the pursuit of knowledge with the onslaughts of oppressive clericalism. The search for truth isn't compatible with repression, and Napoleon dealt the university a calamitous blow in 1811. The vicious Peninsular War led to unprecedented destruction; neither the French nor British forces showed any regard for the historic structures of the city. The French commander Marmont razed much of Salamanca's southwestern district in order to erect defensive breastworks against an antici- pated attack by the British under Arthur Wellesley (later the Duke of Wellington). Dozens of colleges, convents, and churches were totally destroyed Salamanca slid further into decline and never fully recovered. The university no longer ranks among Spain's most prestigious institutions, let alone Europe's.

Even without a world-class university, a visit can be very pleasurable. Thousands of students enliven the streets until the wee hours of the morning. Everyone is attracted to the cafés of Spain's most nearly perfect square, the arcaded Plaza Mayor. The tables and chairs are put outdoors even in the middle of winter, in the hope of taking advantage of even a few minutes of sun- shine. *Sangría* is poured, friends are hailed, plans made, and lives are lived in golden Salamanca.

BARCELONA:
CIUTAT VELLA

Start: Plaça de Catalunya (Metro: Catalunya).

Finish: Museu Frederic Marès, behind the cathedral.

Time: 2 to 3 hours, not including rest stops.

Best Times: Any day from 9am to 1pm and 4 to 7pm April through October, 9am to 2pm November through March.

Worst Times: Monday through Saturday from 1:30 to 4pm, when most shops and other sites are closed; winter evenings after 5pm.

T he city within the walls of Barcino was primarily a commercial and governmental center, not residential. Most of the populace lived in the countryside beyond. Long stretches of the Roman ramparts survive, as do fragments of pagan temples and the foundations of aristocratic homes. The Visigoths and Moors left little physical evidence of their occupations. What dominates the Ciutat Vella—the Old City beside the Mediterranean—today are the churches, palaces, and monuments of the Middle Ages. They are concentrated in the Barri Gòtic (Gothic Quarter), an area 20 times the size of the Roman quarter it encloses. Here is probably the richest concentration of 12th- to 15th-century Gothic architecture to be found anywhere in Europe.

The constricted passages between the buildings in this section screen out the sun except for a few hours each day. However, any potential oppressiveness is eased by the many pocket plazas and a few larger spaces, many of them forcibly carved out of the district by the razing of shabby medieval tenements and the erection of more suitable mansions in their place.

On the east, the Barri Gòtic is delineated by the Via Laietana, a road built through the Old City in 1908 to connect the upper reaches of the city with the harbor. On the west is La Rambla, a boulevard that runs from the waterfront to the Plaça de Catalunya, at the northern edge of the Ciutat Vella. It follows the border of the hated walls imposed on the city in the 14th century by Jaume I, which were eagerly demolished between 1854 and 1865. La Rambla is the bumptious, thumping soul of the city. The prideful Catalans have their own distinctive language, *catalá,* which survived despite four decades of suppression by the autocratic Francisco Franco following the 1936–39 Civil War. The transformation of place names and street signs from Spanish *(castellano)* to *catalá* is essentially complete, although a few obscure sites and pre-1990 street maps may still

East Is South

Orienting oneself in Barcelona can be perplexing. If a line is drawn from the mountains behind the city down to the harbor, it can be seen that the true axis is from the northwest to the southeast. To most residents and tour guides, that is too confusing. They prefer to speak of north or south, east or west, without modification. The problem is that not everyone agrees on which is which. Some sources refer to the main facade of the cathedral, for example, as the "west" side, while others call it the "north" side. So, to align yourself with what seems to be the prevailing view, face the harbor. Call that "south." Then turn around, looking "north." This is the orientation typically used by concierges and guidebooks (including this one).

Ciutat Vella

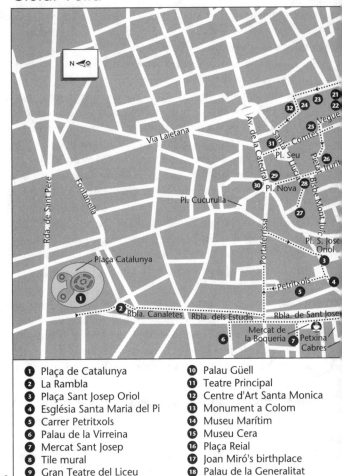

- ❶ Plaça de Catalunya
- ❷ La Rambla
- ❸ Plaça Sant Josep Oriol
- ❹ Església Santa Maria del Pi
- ❺ Carrer Petritxols
- ❻ Palau de la Virreina
- ❼ Mercat Sant Josep
- ❽ Tile mural
- ❾ Gran Teatre del Liceu
- ❿ Palau Güell
- ⓫ Teatre Principal
- ⓬ Centre d'Art Santa Monica
- ⓭ Monument a Colom
- ⓮ Museu Marítim
- ⓯ Museu Cera
- ⓰ Plaça Reial
- ⓱ Joan Miró's birthplace
- ⓲ Palau de la Generalitat

have old designations. Those with a knowledge of Spanish will want to know that *paseo* (boulevard) is *passeig* in *català, calle* (street) is *carrer,* and *plaza* is *plaça.*

● ● ● ● ● ● ● ● ● ● ● ● ● ● ●

Start this walking tour at the center of:

1. **Plaça de Catalunya,** a sweeping four-sided plaza at the edge of the Ciutat Vella. It was created in 1927 to mark the joining of the Old City by the harbor and the Eixample,

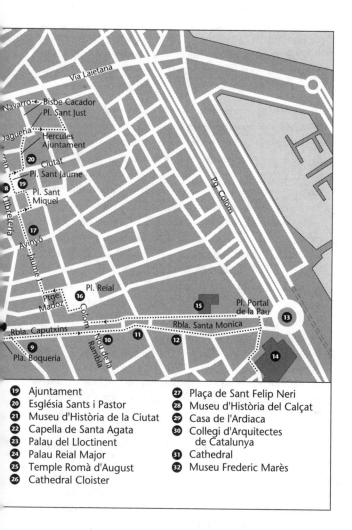

19 Ajuntament	**27** Plaça de Sant Felip Neri
20 Església Sants i Pastor	**28** Museu d'Història del Calçat
21 Museu d'Història de la Ciutat	**29** Casa de l'Ardiaca
22 Capella de Santa Agata	**30** Collegi d'Arquitectes de Catalunya
23 Palau del Lloctinent	**31** Cathedral
24 Palau Reial Major	**32** Museu Frederic Marès
25 Temple Romà d'August	
26 Cathedral Cloister	

the extension of the metropolis undertaken during the second half of the 19th century. It often serves as a stage for loud but usually benign political demonstrations. Clouds of pigeons whirr and flutter around anyone who offers them stale bread or seeds. At the northern side of the plaza are two large fountains. They operate on an unpredictable schedule but are cooling in summer (when functioning) and dramatic at night (when illuminated).

Walk to the southwest corner of the plaza. Across the street is the popular **Café Zurich,** with rows of tables set outdoors in nice weather to enable people to enjoy the outdoor ambience. An underpass leads down to the Metro station and up to the other side; this will bring you to the start of:

2. **La Rambla,** a pedestrian promenade bordered by plane trees and one-way streets on either side. It follows a slightly zigzag route down to the harbor, about a mile away. Beneath the promenade is what remains of the Cagadell River, a sluggish course that was filled in and eventually covered over by the mid-19th century. The Arabic word for "riverbed" is *rambla,* a linguistic vestige of the relatively short stay of the Moors. Sections of La Rambla bear names reflecting the churches, monasteries, and other prominent structures erected along the way. The one here, at the start, is Rambla dels Canaletes. Over to the right is the **Canaletes fountain.** Drinking its water is said to ensure a return trip to Barcelona. Soccer fans and political groups often gather nearby, their vociferous discussions sounding nearly interchangeable. La Rambla's string of large open-sided newsstands begins here, interspersed with kiosks that sell fresh flowers, birds, and pets.

Walking south toward the harbor, pedestrians are likely to encounter three-generation families taking their ritual constitutional known as the *paseo,* sailors on shore leave, scruffy beggars, stylish models, mimes and street musicians, flamboyant transvestites, and living "statues" who paint themselves silver or gold to depict historical personages. There are tarot-card readers and, frequently, a man offering to write any stroller's name on a grain of rice. It is a shifting, exuberant pageant that lasts from early morning until far into the evening.

Walk down the center of the Rambla. Two blocks along on the right, at the intersection with Carrer Carme, is a Baroque church, **Església Betlem,** which has recently been cleaned and might be worth a look inside. On the opposite side of La Rambla is the **Palau Moja,** which was completed in 1789. It stands on the corner of Carrer Portaferrissa. Walk down that narrow, bustling street, with its many clothing and jewelry shops. This is the ancient Barri Gòtic (Gothic Quarter). After four irregular blocks of alleys, turn sharply right on **Carrer del Pi.** At the corner is **Fargas,** a purveyor of tempting chocolates and coffees. This street, together with many others in the barrio, has had its building facades scrubbed and new paving stones laid down; as a result the district is much brighter. A few steps farther along (at number 16) is the enticing **Charcutería la Pineda,** its windows draped with hams and long ropes of sausage. At the end of Carrer del Pí, turn right into:

3. **Plaça Sant Josep Oriol,** one of many hidden squares in the Barri Gòtic. It invites comparisons with Paris's Left Bank counterparts, with spreading shade trees, the small Hotel Jardí, and quirky shops. The best of the shops, **Bolsa,** sells ceramics and folk art. It's next to the hotel entrance, and another door down is:

Take a Break **Bar del Pí,** Plaça Sant Josep Oriol 1 (no telephone). This is a popular gathering spot for neighborhood residents, students, artistic folk, and knowledgeable tourists. Café tables, which are set outdoors in the middle of the plaza in nice weather, often attract street musicians. Coffee with steamed milk and small glasses of red wine or beer are the beverages of choice to accompany the selections of *tapas* and sandwiches. It is open daily from 9am to 9:30pm.

On a raised platform where many of the bar's tables are arranged is a statue of the Catalan poet and playwright, Angel Guimerà, who lived nearby and died in 1924. The square connects with two other small plazas that comprise three sides of a church, the:

4. **Església Santa María del Pi.** Built in a style often described as Catalan Gothic, its boxy, wide-body design is marked by high thick walls, flat-topped towers, and a squat roof. Construction began in the early 14th century and ended in the late 15th century. Walk around to the front, into the adjoining Plaça del Pi, to view the massive rose window above the entrance. This square, with its five orange trees, is often utilized for flea markets and fairs of various kinds. Go to the narrow opening at the northwest corner, where you will find:

5. **Carrer Petritxols,** a short block of surprisingly upscale art and antiques galleries and a couple of homey pastry

shops. The best known and highly influential gallery is the **Sala Parès,** at number 5. Founded in 1840, it was the first Barcelona gallery to exhibit the work of the very young Pablo Picasso. At the end of the alley, turn left on Portaferrissa, cross over to La Rambla, and continue in the same direction as before. On the other side is the:

6. **Palau de la Virreina,** which was commissioned by a corrupt military officer and politician, Manuel d'Amat i de Junyent. Elevated to Viceroy for his services to King Felipe V in Chile and Peru, he moved into this mansion in 1778. Within four years, he was dead, leaving behind his wife, the Vicereine, for whom the structure is named. The interior was long ago stripped to the walls; however, a few rooms on the lower floors are now used for temporary exhibitions.

Continue along the same side of La Rambla a short distance farther until you reach a passage with the remarkable:

7. **Mercat Sant Josep,** a market better known as **La Boquería.** Established in the mid-19th century, the soaring roof of glass and cast-iron fretwork as well as its supporting pillars were added about 50 years later. Plunge into the cacophony of grocers, butchers, and fishmongers tending their stalls while shouting beguilements to prospective patrons. Demanding housewives and chefs from the city's top restaurants prowl the aisles, picking through pyramids of shiny melons and peaches as well as bundles of albino asparagus and baby French beans, poking at glistening heaps of clawed shrimp and slab-sided skate and plump sea bass, squeezing loops of *butifarra* sausages and garlands of garlic. It is both a joyous tumult and a photogenic education in the Spanish culinary repertoire. La Boquería is open Monday through Saturday from 8am to 8pm. If you have been tempted by all this food, you might want to stop by:

Take a Break Bar Pinotxo, La Boquería (tel. 317-1731). A depiction of Pinocchio between the words "Bar" and "Kiosco" is the bar's only identification, since everyone knows about the humble eight-stooled counter and its gregarious manager, Juanito, who presides over the grill. There is no menu, so just point to whatever looks good. The atmosphere is as giddily raucous as the market itself. Pinotxo is open Monday through Thursday from 6am to 5pm, Friday and Saturday from 6am to 8pm. To find the bar, turn right immediately after entering the market from La Rambla.

Leave the market by the main entrance and turn right. After a few steps, at the corner of an alley called Petxina, note the sinuous mosaic that covers the angled storefront of **Antigua Casa Figueras,** a long-established confectioner. Cross over to the center promenade and continue in the same direction down La Rambla. On the left, at the corner of Carrer Cardenal Casañas, an excited metal dragon leaps out over a half-furled copper parasol. He holds a lamp. The shop below was once **Casa Bruno Quadros,** established more than a century ago. It has kept the same mock-Asian decor it had when umbrellas were sold here, but now it is a bank. A few steps farther, you will see, set into the center of the promenade, a colorful:

8. **Tile mural,** installed according to a circular design by Joan Miró. The native Catalan sculptor and painter is honored equally with the two other artists claimed by Catalunya as its own—Pablo Picasso and Salvador Dalí. (Picasso came from Malaga, in the south, and spent only a few early years in Barcelona, whereas Dalí, although born in northern Catalunya, was a monarchist and thus was more loyal to Madrid. Only Miró was a loyal, lifelong Catalan.) There is another, larger mural by Miró on a wall at the airport and a stately outdoor sculpture at the Plaça Espanya, near one of the railway stations. With this mural on La Rambla, near the harbor, the favorite son greets visitors arriving by land, by air, and from the sea.

Over on the right, at the intersection with Carrer Sant Pau, is the:

9. **Gran Teatre del Liceu,** which opened in 1857 as an opera house. Much of it was destroyed by fire in 1861, but it was rebuilt in less than a year after a prodigious fund-raising effort. In 1994, the interior was once again gutted by fire. This time, the initial fervor to rebuild quickly deteriorated into squabbles among divas, musicians, neighbors, Catalan nationalists, and Spanish politicians. An announced plan to complete the renovations by 1997,

Orwell and La Rambla: 1937

George Orwell went to Barcelona as a journalist to cover the Civil War. Caught up in the idealist ardor that drew many intellectuals and artists to take up the Loyalist cause, he joined the militia only days after his arrival. As he later wrote in *Homage to Catalonia*, "when one came straight from England the aspect of Barcelona was overwhelming. Practically every building of any size had been seized by the workers and was draped with red flags or with the red and black flag of the Anarchists; every wall was scrawled with the hammer and sickle and with the initials of the revolutionary parties; almost every church had been gutted and its images burnt. Every shop and café had been collectivized, even the bootblacks had been collectivized and their boxes painted red and black. Waiters and shop-walkers looked you in the face and treated you as an equal. . . . Tipping had been forbidden by law. The revolutionary posters were everywhere. . . . Down the Ramblas, the wide central artery of the town where crowds of people streamed constantly to and fro, the loud-speakers were bellowing revolutionary songs all day and far into the night. . . . In outward appearance it was a town in which the wealthy classes had practically ceased to exist."

After several terrifying, tedious months on the front line, Orwell returned on leave to a changed city. Billeted in a hotel on La Rambla, he observed, "Now the tide had rolled back. Once again it was an ordinary city, a little pinched and chipped by war, but with no outward sign of working-class predominance. The change in the aspect of the crowds was startling. The militia uniform and the blue overalls had almost disappeared; everyone seemed to be wearing the smart summer suits in which Spanish tailors specialize. Fat prosperous men, elegant women, and sleek cars were everywhere . . . the normal division of society into rich and poor, upper class and lower class, was reasserting itself. . . . So nothing happened on 1 May. It was a queer state of affairs. Barcelona, the so-called revolutionary city, was probably the only city in non-Fascist Europe that had no celebrations that day."

the 150th anniversary of the theater, seems unlikely to be realized. In the meantime, the damage is not obvious to passersby since the quietly elegant exterior and lobby weren't affected.

Continue in the same direction on La Rambla and turn right at the next block—Carrer Nou de la Rambla. On the left, at number 3–5, is:

10. **Palau Güell,** a mansion designed by Antoni Gaudí i Cornet for his most prominent patron, the aristocratic industrialist, Eusebi Güell i Bacigalupi. Recent sandblasting has cleaned the grime off the exterior so that one can better see Gaudí's unorthodox use of stonecarving and wrought iron. This was his first major work demonstrating the virtuosity he later brought to the aesthetic movement known as art nouveau in France but described here as *modernisme*—modernism. Güell didn't live here long; the building is now a museum dedicated to memorabilia of Catalan music hall and vaudeville artists. Cross to the opposite side of the street for a glimpse at the 20 fanciful chimneys and ventilators that resemble petrified trees carved by desert winds. (More Gaudí works can be seen in the city, especially in Walk 2.) The museum is open Monday through Saturday from 11am to 2pm.

Return to La Rambla and turn right, staying on the west side. Soon you will arrive at number 27–29 on the right, which is the:

11. **Teatre Principal,** which has recently been renovated. The renovation highlights the ornate neoclassical facade that was added in the mid-19th century to a building constructed in 1778. This is an example of how the lower portion of La Rambla has been upgraded from the deplorable conditions that had prevailed here for decades.

Across La Rambla from the theater is the **Plaça Teatre,** with a white statue of Frederic Soler, a 19th-century poet and playwright who was also an avid Catalan nationalist. Continuing, on the right is:

12. **Centre d'Art Santa Monica,** a frequently recycled building that had previously served as a church, an army barracks, and a museum. It is now an exhibition center for

contemporary art and photography; it is usually open Tuesday through Saturday from 11am to 2pm and 5 to 8pm, but the hours may vary for specific exhibitions.

La Rambla ends in the heavily trafficked Plaça del Portal de la Pau. Out in the middle is the:

13. **Monument a Colom,** an overwrought Victorian extravagance with a 171-foot column surmounted by a statue of Christopher Columbus. His extended arm is pointing off to the south. Fortunately, Columbus the man had a better sense of direction than his sculptor. There is an elevator inside the pillar that goes up to the level of the feet, from which one can view the harbor.

Bear right, crossing the Avinguda de les Drassanes and walking toward the sprawling brick building that is now the:

14. **Museu Marítim** (Maritime Museum). This is one of the least-visited but most impressive structures in a city full of architectural marvels. *Drassana* means "shipyard," and it was built in the 14th century. When it was finished, its seaward bays stood directly on the water. Now the water is almost a quarter of a mile away. Inside, successive rows of arches sweep high over several shipbuilding bays that contain working boats and battlecraft. Perhaps the most impressive exhibit is a glorious replica of the galleon commanded by Don Juan of Austria in his fleet's memorable victory over the Turks at Lepanto in 1571. (That triumph may have contributed to the overconfidence that led to the disastrous defeat of the "Invincible" Spanish Armada only 17 years later.) The museum is open Tuesday through Saturday from 10am to 2pm and 4 to 7pm, and on Sundays and holidays from 10am to 2pm.

If you are energetic, you might like to take a detour along the Moll de la Fusta, the walkway that overlooks the harbor and parallels the boulevard called **Passeig Colom.** From the cafés with indoor and outdoor tables, you can see the cruise ships and pleasure boats that crowd the enclosed port.

Whether or not you take the detour, return to La Rambla and walk north, away from the water. For those who might enjoy this type of museum, you will soon reach the ticket booth, on the right, for the:

15. **Museu Cera,** a wax museum located at the end of the nearby passage. Although it cannot compare with London's Madame Tussaud's, this museum is, at least, open on Mondays, when nearly all of Barcelona's other 40-plus museums are closed.

   Continue up La Rambla, past the Plaça Teatre and its statue, watching for the pedestrian passage on the right called Passatge Colom, with loggias on both sides. It leads into the:

16. **Plaça Reial,** a square enclosed on all sides by buildings of equal height. Too small to be called grand, with a tendency to grow sooty quickly after periodic cleaning, the square still has its attractions. A few years ago, in preparation for the Olympics, it was repaved and steam-cleaned, and the dying palm trees were replaced. The cafés on the east and north sides became popular again. There is a stronger police presence now (which can be seen by the substation on the south side), and this has reduced the number of addicts, drunks, petty criminals, and homeless people who still gather around the square. Look at the center fountain, with its depictions of the Three Graces, and the iron lamps designed by Antoni Gaudí in 1879, before he developed his later, far more distinctive style.

   Bear left across the square toward the western entrance, the Passatge Madoz. There is a new, upscale restaurant in that corner, **Les Quinze Mits,** which is part of the ongoing effort to upgrade the plaza. Beyond the three arches at the end, the passage leads to Carrer Ferran. Opposite the entrance is **Wolf's,** a store with a *modernista* facade of colored glass and Tiffany-like curlicued moldings. Turn right. This is Carrer de Ferran, which was constructed through the Barri Gòtic in the early 19th century to link La Rambla with the government buildings deeper within the quarter. New sidewalks and paving stones were installed after the 1992 Olympics, which make the street appear lighter and wider. Small hotels, bars, and shops of varying types and quality line both sides.

   Three blocks farther will bring you to Carrer d'Avinyó, on the right. A few paces down on the left (at number 7) is **La Manual Alpargatera,** a shop with a white stucco front that specializes in handmade espadrilles in many styles. The canvas-topped shoes with rope soles are worn by dancers of the Catalan folk music, the *sardana,* who perform every Sunday at noon in front of the cathedral. The shop also sells baskets and some items of folk art. It is open Monday through Friday from 9am to 1pm and 5 to 8pm, Saturday from 9am to 1pm.

The women of a brothel reportedly located farther down Carrer d'Avinyó ("Avignon" in Spanish) were said to have inspired Picasso's famous painting *Les Demoiselles d'Avignon.* Completed in 1907, this work is often cited as the start of his involvement in Cubism.

Continue walking along Carrer de Ferran. The next opening on the right is Passatge del Crèdit. Number 4 was:

17. **Joan Miró's birthplace** (1893). There is little to distinguish this building from its neighbors, but the artist eventually inherited the house and used an upstairs room as a studio. The streets to the left of Ferran in this area once comprised the sizable Jewish ghetto known as El Call. The medieval aspect of the neighborhood is still evident in the hunched houses that nearly touch each other above the narrow streets.

Next on the right, past the Hotel Rialto, is the Carrer del Pas de l'Ensenyança, an extravagant name for a short alley that makes a slight jog and then quickly peters out. Walk that way, passing the corner restaurant to enter:

Take a Break La Paraigua, Pas de l'Ensenyança 2 (tel. 302-1131 or 317-1479). Quiet conversation prevails in this subdued *modernista* setting, its ceiling lined in velvet above marble-topped tables. A limited selection of sandwiches and canapés is available: an excellent choice would be a wedge of the firm potato-and-egg omelet called a *tortilla.* Since this establishment is a *whisqueria,* the bartender can mix most conventional cocktails, although most patrons choose beer or wine. The bar is open daily, usually from 11am to midnight.

When you leave the bar, cross the open space in front, bearing left into the bustling **Plaça Sant Jaume.** This was the heart of the old Roman settlement, the intersection of the two main streets that established the quadrilinear grid of the city within its four defensive walls. On the far side, the handsome Catalan Gothic building flying the Spanish and Catalan flags and guarded by stern police officers is the:

18. **Palau de la Generalitat.** This is the seat of the central government of the semiautonomous region of Catalunya, composed of the four provinces in the northeast corner of Spain. Parts of the building date back to the 15th century. A dome on the roof is covered in blue and orange tiles, and above the main doorway is a sculpture of St. George slaying his dragon. Sant Jordi, as he is known in Catalan, is a patron saint of Catalunya, and such images are often meant to invoke his blessing. Inside is a courtyard designed in the High Gothic manner. It is open now only on Sundays between 10am and 1pm, and a written request must be submitted two weeks in advance. At this writing the only exception is on April 23, the Saint's day, when everyone is welcome.

Facing the Generalitat from the opposite side is the:

19. **Ajuntament,** the city hall, parts of which were erected in the 14th century. This physical face-off between the two buildings is more than symbolic. For many years, the regional government has been controlled by the right-of-center Catalan nationalist party, while the city has been administered by a popular Socialist mayor who received much credit for the success of the Olympics.

Walk past the front of the Ajuntament and around the side into Carrer de la Ciutat. Very quickly, on the left, take the Carrer d'Hèrcules. This emerges into the Plaça Sant Just, dominated by the:

20. **Església Sants Just i Pastor,** possibly one of the oldest churches in Barcelona, which may trace back to the early 1300s. Owing to repeated alterations, its exact date is hard to discern or establish.

Walk over to the street at the right-hand corner of the small plaza and take the alley on the left called Baixada del Caçador. This slopes down to Carrer del Sots-Tinent Navarro. Turn left and you can see fragments of the **Roman walls.** They are somewhat changed owing to centuries of intentional destruction, rebuilding, and modification, with Gothic and later intrusions. But they are still an imposing sight. This street arrives at Carrer des Jaume I. Cross the street in front of the Hotel Suizo. At the next corner, turn left (after the hotel) on Baixada de la Llibreteria.

At the next corner, on the right, is the: **Information Office of the Museu d'Història de la Ciutat.** Multilingual clerks can answer questions about the museum, as well as about books, prints, and maps for sale. Turn right at the end of the building onto Carrer de Veguer, and walk past a couple of intriguing antique stores to the second building on the right, the:

21. **Museu d'Història de la Ciutat** (City History Museum). Formerly known as the Casa Clariana-Pedellás, this 16th-century mansion was moved here from another site six blocks away. The three floors above ground are filled with weapons, paintings, and other artifacts (often bearing religious significance) of the various peoples who have lived here at one time or another over the last three millennia— Iberians, Phoenicians, Greeks, Romans, Jews, Moors, and Christian Spaniards. But many visitors are more interested in what is *below* ground. When workers were digging a foundation for the mansion, they unearthed the remains of a large section of a late Roman settlement. One can see their old market, forum, residences, and even a necropolis. The museum is open Tuesday through Saturday, 9am to 8:30pm, Sundays and holidays from 9am to 1:30pm, and Monday from 3:30 to 8pm. As you leave the museum, turn right into the **Plaça del Rei.** This theatrical space is enclosed by high walls. Near this corner is a black metal sculpture by Eduardo Chillida. At your back is the rear of the history museum and on your right is the side of the:

22. **Capella de Santa Agata,** a 14th-century chapel named for a woman who suffered a common martyrdom during the Roman era. When she refused the amorous advances of a high Roman official, she was forced into prostitution and then tortured. When she continued to insist on her virtue, her body was virtually torn apart. Masses are no longer conducted in this chapel, which now serves as an exhibition hall. The chapel is worth a short visit, if only to view the high altar and the retable painting behind it. On your left is the:

23. **Palau del Lloctinent,** a Renaissance palace built for a Catalan viceroy. Now, it houses the royal archives of Aragon, whose monarchs once ruled Catalunya. If the doors are open, you might want to step inside to see a striking coffered ceiling.

On the north side of the square, straight ahead, stands the:

24. **Palau Reial Major,** which has architectural elements dating back to the 13th century but is primarily a product of 15th-century artisans. In the northeast corner of the plaza, a staircase of gracefully curving steps leads up to the entrances to both the Capella de Sant Agata and the hall inside the palace known as the **Saló del Tinell,** which is also used for exhibitions. It is believed that Queen Isabel and King Fernando received Columbus (or "Colón") when he returned from his first voyage either in this hall or on the steps outside. Even if their meeting did not take place here, it would have been fitting; one can easily imagine the pageantry of a formal celebration here. Nowadays, the staircase often serves as a riser for orchestras and choral groups.

Return to the Chillida sculpture and take the Bajada de Santa Clara, passing to the left of the Palau del Lloctinent. Cross the Carrer dels Comtes, entering the Career Pietat, as you pass the rounded end of the cathedral on your right. Take the next left—an alley called Paradis—down to number 10 (on the left), a building owned by the city government. A sign there reads:

25. **Temple Romà d'August.** If the door is open, step inside and walk over to the right. There, behind an iron grate, you can see the bases of fluted columns—the remains of what was probably the majestic temple of Emperor Augustus. They are a ghostly presence.

Then retrace your steps along Paradis, and turn left on Pietat, following the cathedral; enter the (usually) open door ahead and go down the stairs into the:

26. **Cathedral Cloister.** Immediately in front you will see a mossy fountain topped with a small bronze statue of St. George and his hapless dragon. In this courtyard are two surprises: a grove of magnolias and towering sentinel

palms and a pond with a flock of plump geese. The presence of the birds symbolizes the Roman era in Barcelona, presumably after Christianity was adopted.

Circle the vaulted cloister counterclockwise, walking past hundreds of votive candles set in front of side chapels, and return to the street, turning right. You will be on Carrer Bisbe Irurita, where you will pass **Plaça de Garriga i Bachs.** On a wall above a raised platform there is a sculpture by Josep Llimona memorializing the afflictions suffered by the city during the Napoleonic Wars; it depicts priests and aristocrats on their way to be executed by the French. At the end of the plaza, turn left onto Carrer Montjuïc del Bisbe, another gloomy lane that twists down to the right, then left into:

27. **Plaça de Sant Felip Neri.** This compact square, with its barely active six-sided fountain and three feathery plane trees, is deceptively calm. On one side is an elementary school whose pupils periodically run, jump, and shout in the square. On the walls of the school and the adjacent church are dozens of deep pockmarks. They are reminders of the final year of the 1936–39 Civil War, when a bomb fell here and killed 20 children during their recess.

To the right of the entrance to the plaza is one of the city's undeniably esoteric repositories, the:

28. **Museu d'Història del Calçat** (Museum of Antique Footwear). Its two rooms of sandals, conquistador boots, and Victorian high-button shoes may be of interest, and the caretaker will be delighted to provide commentary, although only in Spanish or Catalan. It is open Tuesday through Sunday from 11am to 2pm.

Leave the plaza by the same street, turning left back onto Carrer Bisbe Irurita, which joins Carrer Santa Llúcia from the right. Take a few steps down that street, noting, on the right, the entrance to the **Capella de Santa Llúcia,** a chapel attached to the western wall of the cathedral. Its 13th-century door is pure Romanesque in style, predating by centuries the larger structure to which it is joined. Opposite the chapel is the entrance to the:

29. **Casa de l'Ardiaca** (House of the Archdeacon) completed in 1512. Up a few steps to the wide portal is a pleasing

courtyard with a tile dado as well as fountains and plantings that can be viewed. After a look, return to the corner of Bisbe Irurita and turn right down the ramp. This will take you to the Plaça Nova. As you exit, turn around to look at the **Roman Gate.** Twin cylindrical towers crowd the opening, and a section of the ancient city wall stretches off to the left. The original ramparts were built in the 3rd century. Both the towers and the walls have been significantly altered over the centuries (with clumsy repairs and Gothic insertions), but you can still get an idea of the proportions of the fortified Roman city. (An outer perimeter wall, enclosing a much larger area, was erected during the reign of Juame I in the 14th century, but little of it remains.)

Walk east toward the front of the cathedral, which you can now see. Over to the right is the:

30. **Collegi d'Arquitectes de Catalunya** (College of Architecture). The building itself does not enhance either the plaza or the reputation of the school. But the frieze etched in concrete above the ground floor was based upon drawings by Pablo Picasso.

Continue onto the Avinguda de la Catedral, which used to be clogged with traffic and tour buses rumbling in place like elephants at a water hole. However, in preparation for the '92 Olympics, a huge parking garage was built underground and so virtually all vehicular traffic has been banned here. Now pedestrians can circulate freely and enjoy unobstructed views of the:

31. **Cathedral** ("La Seu" in Catalan). A long stretch of the Roman wall was razed centuries ago to provide space for the plaza immediately in front of the church. On Sundays at noon, musicians with antique instruments usually position themselves on the steps and begin to play the ancient *sardana*. It is haunting music, dominant with oboes and other woodwinds, and alternately somber and spirited. Dancers join hands to form circles in the plaza, their coats and other belongings piled in the middle. The movements of their feet are carefully structured. Anyone can join a circle, but the steps aren't as simple as they might seem to be.

The cathedral was begun in 1298, but most of what you can see from the plaza wasn't completed until the end of

The Travails of Santa Eulàlia

Inside the cathedral is a shrine to Barcelona's copatron saint, Eulàlia. Her story has been told and retold since her death at the hands of the Romans in A.D. 304 Eulàlia had the misfortune of becoming an adolescent when the Roman rulers of Barcelona were making one last effort to impose their pantheon of gods upon the insurgent Christian faith. Young Eulàlia, on a trip to Barcino from her wealthy home village of Sarriá, was reportedly shocked by the venality and licentiousness of the Roman city. Apparently, she communicated her feelings to the authorities, for the Roman governor Dacian decided to make an example of her. He forced her to worship at the altar of the Temple of Augustus. In defiance, Eulàlia refused to make a sacrifice to the pagan dieties; instead, she threw sand at the idols. She was immediately imprisoned. Although only 13 years old, she was apparently quite beautiful, which no doubt exacerbated the subsequent course of events. Dacian imposed a series of sadistic tortures on her (not unlike those suffered by Saint Agata). Eventually, Eulàlia was crucified and, according to some versions of the story, roasted alive. Within the cathedral, a relief panel depicts the nearly nude martyr just before she was put to death.

There is a cult of Santa Eulàlia, complete with miracles and speculations about her origins; her sarcophagus in the crypt of the cathedral is a place of veneration. Actually, historians do not believe Barcelona had an Eulàlia; at best, her story was appropriated from the Roman city of Mérida (in Extremadura) which did have a child-martyr named Eulàlia who defied the Romans, received comparable treatment, and was burned alive in the same year as Barcelona's saint.

the 19th century. Since the original plans were used throughout, there are few marked contrasts in the Gothic exterior to betray the 600-year gap between start and finish. Inside are a few vestiges of the Romanesque style, which was in favor when construction began, but the overall design is Gothic. This cathedral probably replaced two earlier churches and a Roman temple that had successively stood on this site.

If you choose, you could end your walk by visiting the cathedral. It is open daily from 8am to 8:30pm. Otherwise, take the lane to the left of the main facade—Carrer dels Comtes. Soon, on the right, you will come to the entrance to the:

32. **Museu Frederic Marès.** This sculptor bequeathed his substantial collection of medieval art to the city, which is now housed here—a former palace of the ruling Comtes ("Counts") of Barcelona dating back to the 12th century. This museum has more religious carvings and sculptures than most visitors can visually absorb; however, some rooms house such ordinary objects as old coins struck by the Iberians (the earliest known natives of the area) and clothing and toys from the early 20th century. Outside is a restful patio with a fountain encircled by orange trees. The museum is open Tuesday through Saturday from 9am to 2pm and 4 to 7pm, and Sundays from 9am until 2pm.

To return to La Rambla, continue along the same street as far as Carrer Jaume I, turn right through Plaça Sant Jaume, and pick up Carrer Ferran on the other side.

BARCELONA
MODERNISME

Start: Corner of Gran Via de les Corts Catalanes and Passeig de Gràcia (Metro: Passeig de Gràcia).

Finish: Templo Sagrada Familia.

Time: 2 to 3 hours, not including rest stops.

Best Times: Any day from 9am to 2pm and 4 to 7pm April through October, 9am to 2pm November through March.

Worst Times: Monday through Saturday from 1:30 to 4pm, when most shops are closed for siesta; winter evenings after 5pm.

In the mid-19th century, the hated walls that had been built around Barcelona by the Bourbon kings of Madrid were razed. The result was comparable to that of an obese woman suddenly released from her corset. The Barcelonese, who had been bottled up behind their walls since the Roman occupation, spilled out into the countryside in their quest for breathing space. The suburbs and nearby farm villages were swallowed up in the rolling tide and became *barris* of the rapacious city. Most of those towns kept their names—

Sarrià, Sant Gervasi, Horta, Sant Andrew, and Gràcia, among others.

That abrupt explosion of people and construction might have been chaotic, even violent, if it had not been for Ildefons Cerdà i Sunyer. Fortunately for his contemporaries and later generations of Barcelonese, he was asked to draw up a plan for the expansion at the outset.

He had virtually free rein to do what he wanted with miles of generally open land between the old city and the villages that spread across the base and lower slopes of the massif that rises to the north and embraces the present city. Inspired, presumably, by the implementation of Baron Haussmann's redesign of Paris at that time, Cerdà drew up a formal grid of streets running along a roughly north-south axis. A few grand boulevards cut across to provide a touch of visual grandeur and access to the center from distant corners. But most of the streets ran parallel, and the corners of each block clipped off at 45° angles, making the intersections diamond-shaped.

No utopian scheme works out exactly as its originator hopes. Cerdà had intended for each building block to be open at the center, providing inner courtyards and gardens. Some blocks were to be left open, so that all residents would be near a green space. Inevitably, perhaps, developers used up some of the space that had been planned as parks, wringing the last peseta from their investments and leaving many inner courts as dark as the corners of the medieval city to the south. A committed socialist, Cerdà wanted this new city—the Eixample (Extension)—to be thoroughly egalitarian, with working-class families living in the same buildings as merchants and bankers. That didn't happen, either, since the houses of the rich and well-to-do were invariably built to the east of the Rambla de Catalunya, while those of ordinary people appeared to the west.

In spite of these problems and the dissatisfaction of architects who felt unduly constrained by the plan, the Eixample works better than might have been expected. Its streets are bowered with plane trees, the buildings are largely harmonious in style and height, and the entire district somewhat resembles Right Bank Paris.

That Francophilic appearance comes with a pronounced Catalan snap and tang. Cerdà's plan was certified just a couple of decades before the emergence of the movement known here

Modernisme

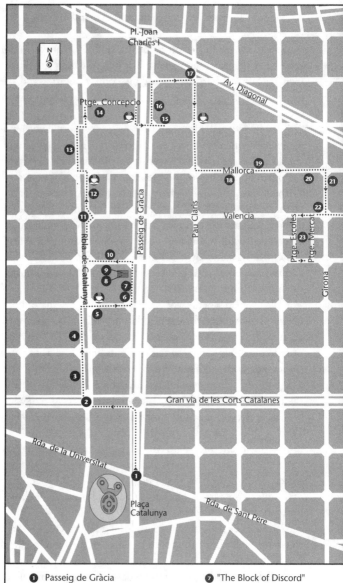

1. Passeig de Gràcia
2. Rambla de Catalunya
3. Casa Jaume Moysi
   Casa Sebastiá Pratjusá
   Casa Climent Asols
4. Casa Rodolf Juncadella
5. Carrer Consell de Cent
6. Casa Lleó Morera
7. "The Block of Discord"
8. Casa Amatller
9. Casa Batlló
10. Fundació Antoni Tàpies
11. Quadrat d'Or
12. Casa Evarist Juncosa
13. Casa Manuel Verdú

Provença

Pl. Mossen
Jacint Verdaguer

Pl. Sagrada
Familia

Pl. Gaudí

Mallorca

Valencia

Passeig Sant Joan

Av. Diagonal

Bailèn

Aragó

Consell de Cent

Gran via de les Corts Catalanes

Sardenya

Marina

Sardenya

Marina

Metro stop ⊖   Restaurant ◖

as *modernisme.* Although it was related to art nouveau in France and North America and to *Jugendstil* or *Secession* elsewhere in Europe, its character was unique to Catalunya. In the last half of the 19th century, architects were seeking new styles of expression, often by combining the conceits of the past in their quest for something fresh. Thus, these neo-everything structures, which brought together elements of Gothic, Greco-Roman classicism, and Byzantine complexities, are seen today throughout western Europe and eastern North America.

Young architects in Catalunya had the same motives, but their results were far different. As will be seen on this tour, such architects as Antoni Gaudí i Cornet and Josep Puig i Cadafalch created sculptures for living and working—free-form organisms sheathed in colorful tiles and intricate stonecarving that resemble surrealistic fairy-tale castles and the lairs of mythical beasts. They are responsible for more than 150 *modernista* buildings, most of them in the Eixample.

This walk focuses on a unique concentration of fantastical structures. Although architecture is the main attraction along this route, there is much to interest shoppers, and numerous cafés and *tapas* bars are available in which to contemplate what the Barcelonese have wrought.

• • • • • • • • • • • • • • • •

Start at the corner of:

1. **Passeig de Gràcia,** opposite the northeast corner of the Plaça de Catalunya. Walk up Gràcia, the city's broadest boulevard, away from the plaza. After 1 block, cross over and turn left on Gran Via de les Corts Catalanes (universally known as "Gran Via"). One block farther, turn right on:

2. **Rambla de Catalunya.** This is an extension of La Rambla, on the south side of the Plaça de Catalunya, with a similar broad tree-lined promenade between one-way streets but with more trendy shops. Umbrellas and awnings shade the tables of sidewalk cafés. At the time Cerdà drew up his plan, this was the right-of-way of a short railroad that ran from the Old City to the town of Sarrià. It quickly became a socioeconomic dividing line, contrary to Cerdà's wishes. Houses to the right of the Rambla were far costlier than those to the left (the "wrong" side of the tracks).

Note the cluster of buildings on the left—at numbers 23, 25, and 27; they are:

3. **Casa Jaume Moysi, Casa Sebastiá Pratjusá, and Casa Climent Asols.** Although they become more interesting at the higher stories (which are filled with detail), they are rather restrained versions of *modernista* design, by younger architects of the second tier.

   In the next block, at number 33, is:

4. **Casa Rodolf Juncadella,** which makes substantial use of sculptural detail on the top floor, while its pediment is lined with eight stone urns. This building was designed by Enric Sagnier i Villavecchia, an architect in great demand during the *modernista* period (about 1890 to 1925). The fact that his style was less radical than that of the period's architectural leaders probably attracted many of his patrons, who wanted to be in vogue but not go to extremes. As will soon be seen, only the most venturesome clients hired the likes of Gaudí and Domènech.

   Turn right on:

5. **Carrer Consell de Cent,** named for the Council of One Hundred which supervised the city government in the Middle Ages. Most of the streets of the Eixample are named either for treasured Catalan institutions or heroes or for the geographical possessions of the once-powerful Aragonese-Catalan empire.

   Some of the streets are called Mallorca, València, Provença (Provence), Còrsega (Corsica), and Sardenya (Sardinia).

   Near the opposite corner is:

   Take a Break   Cerveceria d'Or, Consell de Cent 339 (tel. 215-6439). As the name indicates, the principal drink is beer, with several varieties on draft as well as in bottles. The counter is lined with platters of edibles, from seafood salads to sausages with white beans. Tables are placed outdoors in warm weather. The service is often glum but efficient. The tavern is open daily from 9am to 2am.

   As you leave the tavern, turn left on Consell de Cent. Up high on your left, at the end of the block, there is a bulbous cupola sitting atop eight slender columns, its surface covered with both ceramic tile and deeply carved stone. This is the:

6. **Casa Lleó Morera,** a formerly plain structure before Lluis Domènech i Montaner was commissioned to make alterations in 1902. The facade, which wraps around the corner onto Passeig de Gràcia, is filled with sculptural details, its windows and balconies framed by deep reliefs depicting a variety of creatures and symbols of the new 20th century. You may see griffins and raptors as well as maidens holding a light bulb and camera. The overall effect suggests Arab and Gothic influences without actually employing such classical features as horseshoes or pointed arches.

   Turn left on Passeig de Gràcia for more visual surprises. The row of buildings from here to the next corner is known as *la pomme de discorde* or:

7. **"The Block of Discord,"** though "the apple of discord," carries greater philosophical weight. Besides Domènech's Casa Lleó Morera, two buildings are attributed to Josep Puig i Cadafalch and Antoni Gaudí i Cornet—the triumvirate that dominated the *modernista* movement. On this block the designs of the "Big Three" rather overwhelm those of the prolific but relatively timid Enric Sagnier, at number 37.

   After the Sagnier building comes:

8. **Casa Amatller,** at number 41, notable at first glance for the symmetrically stepped roof comb, reminiscent of the gables of Amsterdam. Many of the decorative details have a neo-Gothic flair, with stone cherubim and animals frolicking around window and door frames. Look for the monkey portrayed as a blacksmith and the rat taking a photo, among others. Polychromed tiles and wrought iron are also used creatively, while much of the surface is a tan and white rendering of the technique known as *sgraffito*.

   Casa Amatller (whose remodeling began in 1898) is the oldest of the *modernista* houses in this Block of Discord. Next door, at number 43, is:

9. **Casa Batlló,** an 1877 building that was extensively overhauled by Gaudí in 1906. It may be the most startling of all

Tibidabo Gives

Walking up the Passeig de Gràcia, you are likely to notice the central peak of the Collserola Hills at the northwestern part of the city. That is Tibidabo, which can be identified by its white basilica and transmission towers. The unusual name is said to come from a Latin phrase meaning "I will give you." The hill does that, for it offers considerable amusement and frivolity with only a smattering of solemnity.

Getting to the top is half the fun. From the metro stop at Avinguda del Tibidabo, cross over to the terminus of the Tramvia Blau. You should have no trouble finding that since the flamboyantly *modernista* building La Rotunda is at the corner. The "Blue Tram," which dates from the turn of the century, may remind you of San Francisco's cable cars. It grinds and waddles up the hill past the giddily exuberant mansions of the wealthy who moved to this slope 100 years ago. With their fanciful admixtures of Gothic, Baroque, Arabist, Byzantine, and Romanesque styles, they are nearly a match for the creations of Gaudí and Domènech down in the Eixample. These buildings are costly to maintain, however, and most have been converted to such other uses as schools, institutes, clubs, and at least one restaurant. At the terminus of the Blue Tram is a plaza with a restaurant, **La Venta,** designed by the famous Catalan Mariscal, and two cocktail lounges, **Merbeyé** and **Mirablau.** The latter establishment has a picture window with stools strategically placed to provide a panoramic view, which can be dazzling at sundown on a clear day. On the plaza is a station for the funicular, which will take you the rest of the way to the summit. It terminates on a terrace just below the basilica, whose base is surrounded by a charming amusement park reminiscent of the late 1920s. On the grounds of the funfair is a small museum of automated devices, including primitive robots. The church beyond has a noted boys' choir that sings daily at 6pm. Tibidabo gives you.

these structure: The front is covered with an intricate mosaic of polished tile fragments that shimmer like tropical coral in the midday sun and when illuminated by floodlights at night. The roofline undulates, evoking the image of a dragon's back; the larger tiles resemble scales, while the shaped stone around the window openings suggest maw, bones, and talons. Probably the tower that looms above the beast is meant to be St. George, the city's patron saint.

A walkway out in the Passeig de Gràcia provides enough distance in case you would like to photograph the Block of Discord; from there, turn left on Carrer D'Aragó, staying on the south side, from which you can view the:

10. **Fundació Antoni Tàpies,** an art museum at number 225, on the opposite side. Designed by Domènech i Montaner, this early brick work is less flamboyant than many of his later creations. Look at the tangle of tubing that rises above the roof. It looks like the concertina wire that protects infantry emplacements, but without barbs. Actually it is a sculpture called "A Cloud and a Chair" by the contemporary artist Tàpies. If you look closely, you can discern a chair outlined by wire sitting stop a "cloud."

Tàpies seems to court controversy, as when he proposed a municipal sculpture depicting a giant sock with a hole in it. Nevertheless, he is regarded in the Catalan art world as the legitimate successor to Picasso and Miró, each of whom has a Barcelona museum specializing in his respective works plus changing exhibits of other contemporary artists. This building's recent rehabilitation was coordinated by the great grandson of the original architect. The museum is open Tuesday to Sunday from 11am to 8pm.

Continue to the next corner and walk up the center meridian of Rambla de Catalunya. This district of the Eixample has been dubbed the:

11. **Quadrat d'Or** (Golden Quadrant) for its trove of *modernista* structures. The works of Gaudí and his colleagues are concentrated along this corridor, extending for two or three blocks on either side of the Passeig de Gràcia. Most of these buildings are now shops and offices, but at least one is a hotel—the Hotel Regente—at the next intersection with Carrer València. Originally the hotel was the:

12. **Casa Evarist Juncosa,** designed by Salvador Viñals i Sabaté. The adjoining building (number 78) was also designed by the same architect. Since these blocks have many interesting visual details, it might be advisable to walk slowly and look closely. At the next corner, down a flight of stairs to the right, is:

☕ **Take a Break**   La Bodegueta, Rambla de Catalunya 100. Wine casks are found at the back bar, and dusty bottles and antique oddities line shelves, enhancing the look of this traditional bodega, or wine cellar. *Cava,* the popular sparkling wine of Catalunya, is featured. A convivial neighborhood crowd pours in and out throughout the day, so it can be almost empty one minute and jammed the next. Small ham or cheese sandwiches are available. The bar is open Monday through Saturday from 7am to 2am.

In the next block, the most appealing of several *modernista* houses are on the left, at numbers 101 and 103. Both are called:

13. **Casa Manuel Verdú,** after the original owner, who commissioned Maurici Augé to design them. Little is known about Augé, not even his birth and death dates. His use of wrought iron and sculptural embellishments is more polished than may be seen on other nearby modernist buildings.

Cross Carrer Provença. Half a block ahead, turn right down the mews called:

14. **Passatge de la Concepció.** Toward the end of the 19th century, a handful of these lanes were created in the Eixample, where you will see small carriage houses. Some are still fashionable residences. Near the far end is the trendy:

☕ **Take a Break**   El Tragaluz, Passatge de la Concepció 5 (tel. 487-0196). The interior of this restaurant reflects the work of contemporary Catalan designers, especially the increasingly famous Mariscal, whose work is in demand all over the city. Beyond the front bar is a room where they serve lighter and faster foods, especially salads, sandwiches, and pastas. This dining area, called **Tragarapid,** is open daily from 1:30pm to 2am.

As you leave the restaurant, turn right, then right again, and proceed half a block down to the corner of Carrer Provença. Directly across the street is the most striking *modernista* edifice yet:

15. **Casa Milà,** also known as "La Pedrera" (The Stone Quarry). The nickname was adopted since the billowing, undulating surface of the facade is made of cut limestone, not poured concrete. Although the architect Antoni Gaudí could have chosen concrete, he preferred to utilize the skills of Catalan ironmongers, stonecarvers, ceramicists, and stained glass and related craftsmen. Casa Milà has been cleaned and renovated in recent years.

If Casa Batlló represents a dragon, Casa Milà must be its undersea dwelling. The building's seven stories wrap around the northeast corner of Gràcia and Provença; each floor has an overhang that waves and curls as if it were being seen through water. The balcony railings seem to resemble clumps of seaweed. On the roof are Gaudí's trademark ventilators and chimneys, some looking like medieval knights, while others form twisted columns. To get a better view, you may want to climb up or take the elevator (if it is working). Groups assemble in the interior court for guided tours in English and other languages. The visiting hours vary; on my last visit, tours were scheduled Tuesday through Saturday at 10am, 11am, and 1pm.

Next to Casa Milà (at numbers 94 and 96) are the somewhat older:

16. **Casa Josep Codina and Casa Ramon Casas,** both designed by Antoni Rovira i Rabassa. Admittedly overshadowed by their flamboyant neighbor, these buildings would receive more attention if they were situated elsewhere. The second casa formerly belonged to the wealthy and influential painter Ramón Casas i Carbó (1866–1932). After prolonged study in Paris, Casas became a leader in the Barcelonese art community. The building is now occupied by Vinçon, a prominent department store that sells furniture and household objects of contemporary Catalan design.

Turn around and walk back up the Passeig. You should be able to see the mountain called Tibidabo, topped by a granite basilica that is illuminated at night. After 2 blocks, the Passeig intersects with Avinguda Diagonal, which, as the name suggests, angles across the grid of the Eixample. Turn right, staying on the near side of Diagonal. At the next corner of that wedge-shaped block is the:

17. **Palau Baró de Quadras,** designed by Puig i Cadafalch, which now houses the Museu de la Música. Unless you are interested in music history, you will probably be more intrigued with the exterior of this building. As with his Casa Amatller in the Block of Discord, Puig mixes robust, deeply carved Gothic fancies with elements borrowed from northern European architecture (for example, dormers that appear to have been copied from an alpine lodge).

Turn right on Carrer Pau Claris. In the middle of the next block is another entrance to Vinçon, the department store. At the corner of Carrer Provença is:

Take a Break Marisquería O'Nabo de Lugo, Pau Claris 169 (tel. 215-3047). Clean and modern, this restaurant specializes in seafood prepared in the Galician manner, from the northwest corner of Spain. Fresh oysters are opened to order. As is true for many restaurants in Spain, *tapas* and drinks consumed at the bar are cheaper than the same items consumed at a table. Open Monday to Saturday from 1 to 4pm and 8:30pm to midnight.

Continue down Carrer Provença and then turn left on Carrer Mallorca. Within 1 block, at number 278 on the right, is another building by Domènech i Montaner, the:

18. **Palau Ramon de Montaner,** which is now a regional government office. Once again, the heaviest, most ornate sculptural depictions (of fish and eagles) are crowded up near the top. In this case, it happened because another architect designed the first two floors. Visitors are permitted to go inside on Saturdays only, from 10am to 1pm. The foyer is worth looking at because of the dazzling use of stained glass and a truly grand staircase.

In the middle of the next block, at number 291–293 on the left, is another Domènech, the:

19. **Casa Thomas.** The architect designed this building for an extended family who were in the engraving business. Originally it consisted of only two stories; later the upper three floors were added by Domènech's son-in-law. Since it is difficult to discern two distinct styles, probably the two men worked together on the addition to maintain the integrity of the facade, which is thickly decorated with carvings and tiles. Presently a furniture design firm occupies the basement level, which can be seen from the street.

    In the next block, on the right, are two houses of the same name:

20. **Casa Dolors Xiró** (at numbers 302 and 304) which also makes use of the familiar *modernista* materials and motifs. Take the next right, onto Carrer Girona. At number 122 is:

21. **Casa Jeroni F. Granell,** which varies the modernist stratagems somewhat with stylized pale-green leaf patterns painted on the facade. A more notable building at the next corner (València) is the:

22. **Casa Eduardo S. Lamarind,** at number 113. Designed by Domènech, it extends the botanical theme with three balustraded balconies, featuring limestone blossoms that frame women with flowing hair holding shields.

    Cross over València, take a few steps to the right, and turn left into the:

23. **Mercat Concepció.** Although this market cannot equal the landmark La Boquería on La Rambla (see Walk 1), it has a similar boisterous atmosphere and careful displays of produce. This is a neighborhood market, somewhat like those at other strategic locations around the city. You can see here some of the vegetables, fruits, seafoods, and meat that will soon be consumed throughout the district.

    Exit back onto València and turn right; after 1 block turn left onto Carrer Bailen. After another block turn right to the intersection of Avinguda Diagonal and Passeig de Sant Joan, which is called the Plaça Mossen Jacint Verdaguer to honor a priest and revered Catalan poet.

    Negotiate the zigzag crossing of the plaza and pick up Carrer Mallorca once again on the other side. At that corner (number 108 Passeig de Sant Joan) is:

24. **Casa Macaya,** another mansion by Puig i Cadafalch. Although this one has a bank on the ground floor, the exterior has not been significantly modified. Puig, who was often considered a contemporary of Gaudí and Domènech, was actually about 20 years younger. His rivals both died in the early 1920s, whereas Puig lived until 1957.

    As you continue on Mallorca, you will be able to see the steeples of a most unusual church. They should hold your interest along the next 3 somewhat uninteresting blocks. After you pass a park on the left, you will arrive at the west end of the:

25. **Templo Expiatori de la Sagrada Familia,** the unfinished masterwork of Antoni Gaudí. Since this end of the church is still under construction, walk another block, cross the street, and then turn left.

    Your first impression might well be that someone took a giant blowtorch to the front. The dark stone seems to be melting, the lintels dripping, the steeples softening. This intricate work has been achieved by Gaudí's cherished stonecarvers. If you look closer, you will see that much more is going on here. The architect was a deeply religious man with a scholarly bent. He ordered sculptures of 30 kinds of plants to be affixed to the facade; each plant grows in both Catalunya and the biblical lands. Above the central portal is a stone representation of a cedar. The tree is green and doves fly around and out of it. Gaudí often used color where none is usually expected. At the top of the four elongated conical steeples are brilliant ceramic starbursts in crimson and gold.

    Examining the facade can take quite awhile, since you will become aware of more and more details. After you take it all in, walk to the corner and turn left on Carrer Provença. Here you will see elements of the walls designed by Gaudí's predecessor. They are more conventional in outline. There is no roof, and what appears to be a permanently emplaced T-shaped construction crane shares airspace with the steeples. At the other end of the church, turn left on Carrer Sardenya. This is the entrance to the church, which is open daily from 10am to 6pm; there is an admission charge.

    When Gaudí died in 1925, he left only a few drawings and vague sketches of his plans for the Sagrada Familia. His assistant Domènech Sugranes i Gras carried on for another 10 years, but money for the project was drying up and then the Civil War began. Work on the church stopped. The country suffered a long period of impoverishment, and little was done with the Templo.

Now, work has picked up again, with the hope of completing the church in less than another 50 years. Having witnessed the quality of the work being done on this facade (whose theme is the Crucifixion), those in charge might wish to save themselves time and money. Controversial as Gaudí undeniably is, there appears to be broad consensus about this new work being undertaken in his name. The sculptures on this wall are egregiously inept, the sort of thing that might be acceptable to philistine totalitarian rulers of remote desert kingdoms. The Roman soldiers look like Star Wars storm troopers, and the groups of figures positioned around the wall seem to be unconnected to the central event. The only noteworthy aspect of Christ on the cross is the fact that he is without the usual loincloth, naked. This cannot be adjudged a step forward in ecclesiastical art. The debate over Gaudí's genius (or his wrong-headedness) and the efforts to complete his visions (or grind them into something less than mediocrity) are likely to continue into the indefinite future. But this is Barcelona's Eiffel Tower, its Statue of Liberty, its Tower Bridge. It will survive.

There is a Metro station at the corner of Provença and Sardenya.

BARCELONA: RIBERA AND CIUTADELLA

Start: Plaça d'Urquinaona (Metro: Urquinaona).

Finish: Parc de la Ciutadella.

Time: 2 hours, not including rest stops.

Best Times: Any day from 9am to sundown, but especially weekends.

Worst Times: After sundown.

A mountain called Montjuïc broods over the southwestern edge of Barcelona harbor. It impeded the spread of the medieval city in that direction, so development took the easier route—along the waterfront in the opposite direction. The district that is east of the old Roman walls but within the extensive 13th-century fortifications is called Ribera. This neighborhood is every bit as lively as the Barri Gòtic, if less monumental, and has survived repeated assaults by expansionist Castilian kings and modern-day urban planners.

In the 18th century Felipe V wanted to enhance the strategic military position of Barcelona begun by Jaume I of Aragon

Ribera and Ciutadella

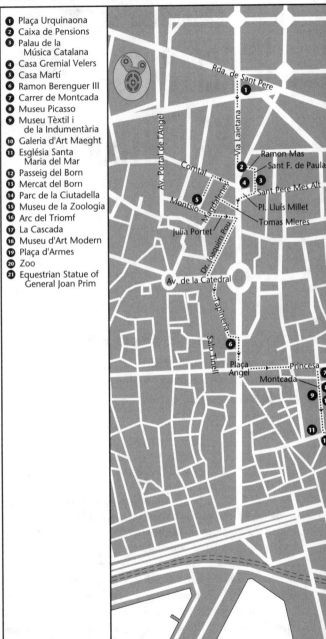

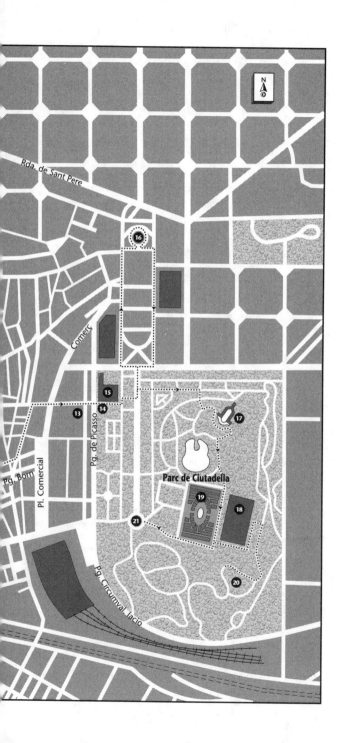

five centuries earlier. He tore down much of Ribera, including monasteries and hundreds of dwellings, in order to construct a huge fortress—the Citadel—which covers about 270 acres. It remained intact until the 1880s, a detested symbol of Madrid's power. Another blow to Ribera followed in 1908, when an avenue called Via Laietana was cut through to the harbor, separating Ribera from the rest of the old city.

The barri languished, its wealthy and middle-class residents moving to the Eixample or the suburbs and its narrow streets becoming more squalid. In the late 1960s and 1970s, a few hopeful breaths of fresh air wafted down those dark alleys. Some of the 14th- and 15th-century mansions and townhouses built by merchants and aristocrats were rediscovered. Three of them were rehabilitated to house a large collection of works donated by Pablo Picasso and his admirers, and another became a textile museum. Later, a market building was converted to a performance space, and numerous bars and informal restaurants opened.

● ● ● ● ● ● ● ● ● ● ● ● ● ● ● ● ●

Begin this tour at the metro station at the southwest corner of:

1. **Plaça d'Urquinaona,** a triangular square one block east of the Plaça de Catalunya. At that point Carrer Pau Claris, to the north, becomes Via Laietana, (named for the native tribes who populated the area when the Romans arrived). Cross over to Laietana, staying on the left side, and walk toward the harbor. At the next street, near the entrance to another metro station, look up at the building on the corner. It is a savings bank:

2. **Caixa de Pensions,** without the usual bank-like sobriety. One of the busiest *modernista* architects, Enric Sagnier, created this curious amalgam of Gothic, Arabic, and Romanesque motifs.

   The street branching off to the north from Laietana on the left at this juncture is Carrer de les Jonqueres. Cross this street, bearing right, and shortly thereafter turn left, into Carrer Ramon Mas. Straight ahead, the brick building with the cylindrical tower is the:

3. **Palau de la Música Catalana,** the supreme achievement of the *modernista* luminary Domènech i Montaner. The concert hall may not look especially remarkable from this angle; much of what you can see here is modern—a restoration and expansion to include music studios and classrooms. Through the doors straight ahead are the ticket booths, and over to the right is a bar. Sometimes when no rehearsals are in progress, visitors can go inside for a casual look. Otherwise, the only way to see the building is to attend a concert or take an irregularly scheduled tour. (Your hotel concierge should be able to obtain pertinent information for you.)

The interior—the concert hall itself—is almost beyond one's imagination. A giant stained-glass bowl bellies down from the ceiling—the most dramatic source of natural light, since most of the walls are of pinkish glass. A lavishly sculptured proscenium frames the stage, with a large bust of the composer Josep Anselm Clavé on the left and one of Beethoven on the right. Overhead, the winged horses of Wagner's Valkyries are frozen in flight, straining toward the leafy tree rising above the head of Clavé.

To gain a better sense of the unusual nature of the building, leave the ticket lobby, turn left, then left again so that you can see the imaginative facade. This isn't easy because of the proximity of nearby buildings. The best place from which to see the building is opposite the far corner, where you can look up at bands of mosaics and composers' busts, at the statue of the nude woman and knight bursting from the prow of the building, and at multicolored pillars whose tops burst into clumps of carved vegetation.

That street where you should be standing is Sant Pere Més Alt. Walk back in front of the Palau to Laietana and cross over. As you look back at the Palau, you will also see:

4. **Casa Gremial Velers,** an 18th-century artisans' guildhall, with a tan-and-white etched facade exemplifying the technique called *sgraffito*.

Walk back up 1 block on Laietana and turn left into Carrer de Comtal. On the left, where Comtal begins, is a new restaurant:

Take a Break   Brasserie Gurnetty, Carrer de Comtal 32 (tel. 301-7397). Relax with a beverage and a *tapa* selected from the platters displayed at a five-sided bar in the center of the room. It's open from noon to 11pm.

Stroll along Comtal, allowing time to glance at the shop windows. You might be amused at the unusual degree of specialization at one shop—**Casa de Bacalao**—at number 8. They sell nothing but codfish. Cooks from the Basque region of north-central Spain are known to boast that they have a cod recipe for every day of the year. In a nation of seafood lovers, cod is the most popular fish of all.

After a few short blocks, Comtal emerges into a broader and busier shopping street—Avinguda Portal de l'Angel. Turn left. A branch of one of the two major department store chains, **Galerías Preciados,** is over on your right. After 1 block, turn left into another narrow street that was recently repaved—the Carrer de Montsió. Shortly, on the left, you will come to:

5. **Casa Marti.** There is a sign for the ground floor restaurant, **Els Quatre Gats.** The building has a double attraction. First, it was designed by Josep Puig i Cadafalch, one of the three major architects of the *modernisme* movement. This building looks like a fortified Gothic mansion, which is entirely fitting here. A Puig trademark—a sculpture of St. George dispatching the luckless dragon—graces the corner above the adjoining iron gate.

The second attraction is the restaurant, "The Four Cats," which was a gathering place for the intelligentsia and artists of the early 1900s. Writers, poets, painters, and theater people met here to test concepts and argue esthetics. Among them, at one time or another, were Miguel Utrillo, Pablo Picasso, Joan Miró, Ramón Casas, and Santiago Rusinyol. Poetry readings, musical performances, and art exhibits were staged. Quatre Gats was the talk of the town, but its legend far outstrips the reality. The original restaurant lasted only six years, from 1897 to 1903. Several years ago, however, it was reestablished with some of the original decor, including a painting of one of the original managers on the back of a bicycle built for two. Pere Romeu was a physical fitness enthusiast; he enjoyed cycling, fencing, rowing, hiking, and even swimming in the Mediterranean in January. He died of tuberculosis soon after he was obliged to close The Four Cats.

Proceed along Montsió (which soon becomes Julia Portet) back to Via Laietana. Turn right on Laietana, and immediately bear right on Carrer Dr. Joaquim Pou, which angles off Laietana. When you reach the pedestrian plaza called Avinguda de la Catedral (the **Hotel Colón** is at that corner), go left of the Museu Diocesà, straight ahead, onto Carrer de Tapineria, which was once a street of cobblers. On the right you can see remnants of the old Roman walls. You will soon reach a statue of:

6. **Ramon Berenguer III,** a 12th-century king of no particular distinction. The open space behind him, though, will give you an excellent view of the Roman wall and its subsequent modifications. Bear right, following the wall, into the small Plaça Angel in front of the **Hotel Suizo.** Cross Laietana and proceed along Carrer de la Princesa. This is actually the main street of Ribera, which has a great many ordinary, utilitarian shops. An unusual one is **El Rey de la Magica,** at number 11, on the left, which has been selling magic tricks and apparatus since 1881.

Continue walking along Carrer de la Princesa; after passing four streets on the right, turn right into:

7. **Carrer de Montcada.** Barely wide enough to allow two horsedrawn carts to pass, this is the most remarkable street in Ribera. Both sides are lined with mansions formerly owned by minor aristocrats and well-to-do merchants between the 13th and 17th centuries. They are built right up to the edge of the property line, and thus loom over pedestrians. Since these buildings are dark with grime and have been neglected for many years, few people have been motivated to glance up or consider what might lie behind those walls.

This street was rediscovered when a local art patron gave the city a major collection of Picasso's youthful drawings, prints, and paintings on the condition that a separate museum be established to house them. Picasso was amenable to these plans despite his hatred of the Franco dictatorship and his self-exile to France. The:

Spain's Red Gold

Saffron is the costliest spice in the world, and Spain produces 70% of the total annual crop. That's fewer than 10,000 pounds, which is understandable, since the crimsom gossamer threads are the dried stigma of a single subspecies of flower—*Crocus sativus.* The fall harvest season lasts only three weeks, during which time the crocus growers must work around the clock since the flowers must be picked the same day they bloom. Each blossom has only three stigmas, barely an inch long. For all the intensive labor to harvest, sort, and dry the flowers, a single farmer averages a yearly harvest of perhaps 2 pounds.

A gram of saffron, about $1/28$th of an ounce, costs about $3 to $6 at a New York specialty food shop. For that reason, few North Americans are familiar with the spice except as a coloring agent—it turns the rice in *paella* yellow. Yet saffron has a distinctive flavor, smelling faintly of must, that is released only when used in larger amounts (for example, a half-teaspoon in a recipe serving four to six people).

There is no better way to experience this exotic taste sensation than to buy a supply of saffron while in Spain. One of the best sources is here on Carrer de la Princesa, at number 38, a few steps beyond the entrance to Carrer Montcada, where the Picasso Museum is located. The shop is called **Angel Jobal.** You can detect aromas from the shop while still a block away, since they also sell many intensely flavorful teas and spices in bulk. A typical herb-size jar of saffron would probably $8 to $12. Another good buy would be any of the Spanish paprikas, which are far more pungent than what is normally available in North America.

8. **Museu Picasso** was opened in 1963 in one of the mansions on the left. As works donated to the museum multiplied, many from Picasso himself, a second connecting mansion and then a third were added. Those who dislike Picasso's later works will be interested to see that he

began as a fairly conventional academic artist. Even those who care little about art would probably enjoy walking through the buildings' interiors, with their spacious inner courts, loggias, and staircases. The museum, one of the most visited sites in Barcelona, is open Tuesday through Saturday from 10am until 8pm, and Sunday from 10am until 3pm. It has a new café that is quite popular.

Across the street from the main entrance to the Picasso Museum, at number 12, is the:

9. **Museu Tèxtil i de la Indumentària,** which is devoted to textiles, one of Barcelona's leading industries for centuries. Opened in 1969 in the 14th-century Palau de los Marqueses de Llió, it takes full advantage of its proximity to the Picasso. Its exhibits are of a somewhat specialized nature—largely fabrics and fashions, including priestly garments. It has an interesting gift shop and café.

The museum is open Tuesday through Saturday from 9am to 2pm and 4:30 to 7pm, Sunday from 9am to 2pm.

Take a Break Tèxtil Cafè, Montcada 12–14 (tel. 268-2598). Tables in the open courtyard provide a retreat from the crowds of the Picasso Museum and invite one to study the structure of this 14th-century building. Vestiges of numerous earlier renovations, such as closed doorways and walled-up windows, illustrate that these buildings are living organisms, always changing. Espresso, soft drinks, wine, and beer supplement the short list of snacks and desserts, including raisin-and-pinenut cake, salads, and sandwiches. There is never any pressure to vacate a table. The café is open Tuesday through Sunday from 10am to midnight.

Leave the café and turn right along Montcada. Beyond the Museu Picasso, on the left, another *palau* houses the prestigious:

10. **Galeria d'Art Maeght,** which promotes contemporary artists by holding frequent temporary exhibitions of their work. The building, which dates from the 16th century, has been altered very little, unlike most of the other mansions on the street. Admission is free, and the gallery is open

Tuesday through Saturday from 9:30am to 2pm and 3 to 8pm.

Continuing along Montcada, admirers of folk art might want to browse in a small shop on the right, **Populart,** which features Latin American crafts. At the end of Montcada, turn right. Up ahead are steps leading into the:

11. **Església Santa Maria del Mar.** Built entirely in the 14th century, this is perhaps the most beloved church in Barcelona and certainly much admired for its pure statement of the Catalan Gothic style. It is solid, even ponderous, outside, while the interior exemplifies the daring of the architects and stonecutters of the time. They gambled on widely spaced columns that no 20th-century counterpart would attempt—at least, not without the security of steel reinforcement. The result is a space of powerful impact, of rare simple grandeur.

Unfortunately, owing to vandalism and theft, the caretakers have instituted limited visiting hours. Unless a mass or a concert is scheduled, the doors are likely to be locked. From the church, walk east along the:

12. **Passeig del Born,** which is as much plaza as street. It has served many purposes over the years; in medieval times, it was the heart of the city, the venue for jousts and fairs. The workshops of guildsmen were clustered here and on neighboring streets. Most of the buildings now standing date from the 18th and 19th centuries. Since the early 1980s many of them have been converted into trendy bars and cafés that cater to evening crowds. In case you would like to return for after-dinner drinks, several of note include: **Miramelindo** (number 15), **Berimbau** (number 17), and **Copetín** and **Vis a Vis** (both at number 19).

At its eastern end, the Born emerges at the Plaça Comercial. Dominating the opposite side is the:

13. **Mercat del Born,** a large, shed-like, ironwork structure dating from the Victorian era. The roof is covered in angular patterns of green-and-orange ceramic tiles. Once the largest market in Spain (and possibly the world), it is now used, somewhat ineffectually, for periodic live performances and other cultural or community events.

Turn left on Plaça Comercial, which becomes Carrer del Commerç. After 2 blocks, turn right on Carrer de la Princesa. The next street is Passeig de Picasso; cross over. Ahead you will see:

14. **Parc de la Ciutadella.** This is where the mammoth citadel of Felipe V stood until the late 19th century. Its destruction and subsequent conversion of the land to a public park was celebrated by the World Exposition of 1888, one of several key events that have transformed the city over the past 150 years. Several of the remaining attractions highlighted for this walk were built for the Exposition, without any plans for their continued existence.

After you enter the park, the building to your left is now the:

15. **Museu de la Zoologia.** Domènech i Montaner embodied the *modernisme* movement. He was commissioned to create a **Café-Restaurant** to complement his **Hotel Internacional.** With an unprecedented 1,600 rooms the hotel opened only three months after the first spadeful of earth was turned. (By contrast, the largest hotel in Barcelona today has about 500 rooms.) Despite the stupendous effort made to construct the hotel, it was demolished at the end of the Exposition. The Café-Restaurant, on the other hand, which wasn't finished in time, has survived. It looks like a parody of a medieval fortress, with towers, battlements, and escutcheons with fictitious heraldic symbols of flora and fauna. Although the building is largely brick (considered at the time a humble construction material that should be covered over), there is a band of flashy ceramic tiles near the roofline. Turn left at the other side of the building for a look at the facade, especially the elaborately decorated tower up on the right, with its fanciful wrought-iron weathervane.

The interior display of stuffed animals and live and dead bugs may be of only limited interest. Turn right and continue straight ahead (east); as you cross an untrafficked road, pause a moment and look to your left. In the distance, beyond the entrance gates and at the far end of a palm-lined ceremonial promenade called the Passeig Lluís Companys, is an:

16. **Arc del Triomf.** Josep Vilaseca favored the neo-Mudejar style developed by Arab artisans who remained in Spain after the final victory of the Catholic kings in 1492. The arc was renovated for the 1992 Olympic Games, as was the Passeig Lluís Companys.

    Continue walking in the same direction, bearing slightly left, and pick up the path that cuts across the northern edge of the park. Ahead you can see a modern sculpture consisting of large metal gears. About 70 yards beyond the sculpture, another path veers off to the right; take that path and notice a bandstand coming into view ahead. To your left is a wondrously overwrought fountain called:

17. **La Cascada.** In front is a moat and a large pool embraced by twin monumental staircases that curve upward to meet at a pavilion at the rear. Pedestals support statues of mermaids, winged and rearing horses, and fierce griffins with water spouting from their mouths. Vertical fountains bracket the waterfall spilling down from a sculptured grotto at the top. Critics routinely dismiss La Cascada as pompous; however, its excesses do provide some unintended humor. The cascade was extensively renovated before the Olympics and has once again become an important gathering place for Barcelonese. Impromptu *sardanas* often start up in the plaza in front of the fountain.

    Turn your back to the Cascade and face the small lake beyond, which is often filled with rented rowboats on pleasant days. Take the path to the left of the lake (marked by a life-sized concrete rendering of a woolly mammoth). Through here, the palm fronds are full of wild *cotorras* (a kind of parakeet). After you pass a small children's playground, bear to the left, toward the buildings now coming into view. The first of these is the:

18. **Museu d'Art Modern,** ensconced in what was formerly an arsenal for the Bourbon Citadel. Converted to various uses since its construction in 1727 (including a military barracks and, briefly, a royal residence), it now shares space with the Catalan Parliament. The museum specializes not in modern art (as the term is usually understood) but rather in the paintings, sculptures, and decorative arts of Catalans associated with *modernisme* and related movements. Since

Montjuïc

Barcelona honors its great artists while they are still alive. Besides the museums devoted to Picasso and Tàpies (see Walk 2), there is the **Fundació Joan Miró,** situated on **Montjuïc,** the hill that dominates the western end of the harbor. Its name is believed to mean "Mountain of the Jews," for the presumed presence of a Jewish cemetery. An earlier theory held that it was the site of a temple to the Roman god Jupiter, also known as Jove.

Apart from a castle erected on the summit in 1640, nothing much was done with the hill until the early 1900s. The success of the 1888 Universal Exposition inspired talk of a sequel, and it was proposed that the base and lower slopes of Montjuïc be used for that purpose. After repeated delays, the business community and municipal authorities agreed on 1929. Extensive landscaping transformed the mostly barren promontory into a park with groves of trees and lavishly planted gardens.

One of the buildings erected for the 1929 World's Fair that has survived is the neo-Baroque National Palace, which has subsequently served as a museum of Catalan art. Nearby is the **Poble Espanyol,** a mock "village" with replicas of exemplary everyday architecture from various Spanish towns and villages and a fortified wall resembling those of Avila. The Poble Espanyol has recently been rejuvenated, with the addition of restaurants, taverns, and nightclubs. The **Pavelló d'Alemanya** (German Pavilion) designed by Mies van der Rohe for the 1929 fair has been reconstructed from drawings and photographs. It was in the original structure that the famous Barcelona chair was introduced. Montjuïc also has a military museum (in the castle), an Olympic stadium and natatorium, the exhilarating **Palau d'Esports Sant Jordi** designed by the Japanese architect Arata Isozaki for the '92 Games, an amusement park, an open-air Greek theater, museums of archeology and ethnology, and the Miró museum—a contemporary building eminently suited for the paintings and sculptures of the lyrical surrealist.

other museums are scheduled to open in more central parts of the city, the future of this one is uncertain.

In front of the Museu d'Art Modern and Parliament is the:

19. **Plaça d'Armes,** a square landscaped in the formal French manner with clipped hedges and neat flowerbeds. In the center, set on a pedestal in the middle of an ornamental pool, is the milky white marble sculpture of a nude woman almost swooning into the water, her hair flowing over her face and shoulder. Created by Josep Llimona in 1907, its title translates as *Disconsolate* or *Despair*. This is a copy of the original.

Walk past the Museum-Parliament building and bear left. Within a short distance you will see the entrance to the:

20. **Zoo.** Actually this zoo does not measure up to its better-known counterparts elsewhere, but children may enjoy the section designed for them. It has an aviary that can be entered, a petting compound, a row of cages with rabbits, playground equipment, and a snack bar. A particular favorite of all visitors is *Snowflake,* an aging albino gorilla. At the western end of the fenced zoo grounds is an aquarium with a pool for performing dolphins and a killer whale. Zoo hours are 10am to 5pm in winter, and 9:30am to 7:30pm in summer.

Exit the Zoo where you entered and walk back past the southern edge of the Plaça d'Armes into the traffic circle beyond. In the middle is an:

21. **Equestrian Statue of General Joan Prim.** A popular figure in the mid-19th century for his support of Catalan causes, Prim served briefly as military governor of Barcelona. Two years into what is described as the "Glorious Revolution of 1868," he handed over the Citadel to the civilian government. Since that gift eventually resulted in this park, it is a fitting location for his monument.

On the traffic circle is a scheduled stop of the **Bus Turístic.** This special bus travels a circular route past many of the city's prominent attractions, making 15 stops. Those who purchase half- or full-day tickets can get on and off any bus numbered 100 as often as desired. Buses run every 20 to 30 minutes between 9am and 9:30pm. The route begins at Plaça de Catalunya. Tickets are available from mid-June to mid-October.

If the bus is not available, walk to Passeig de Picasso and hail a taxi or else walk west on Avinguda del Marques de l'Argentera down to the waterfront.

Madrid: La Ciudad Antigua

Start: Puerta del Sol (Metro: Sol).

Finish: Plaza Mayor.

Time: 2 hours, not including rest stops.

Best Times: Any day from 9am to 1pm and 4 to 7pm April through October, 9am to 3pm November through March.

Worst Times: August, when every resident who can afford to do so leaves the city. Siesta periods (usually 1:30 to 5pm), when most shops and attractions are closed; winter evenings after 5pm.

In a sense, Madrid is an artificial city, a royal whim, a 16th-century anticipation of the District of Columbia or Brasilia without organic reasons of topography or natural resources to justify it. Although a small settlement had existed beside the sluggish Manzanares River for centuries, where the Moors established a lightly fortified outpost in the 9th century, Mayrit (as it was called) remained just an insignificant village until Felipe II made a crucial decision. Noting Mayrit's location near the geographical center of the Iberian Peninsula,

70

he decided to make it his capital. He wanted to counteract the centrifugal forces of the separatist regions on the periphery of his fractured land by establishing a central authority where none had existed. His plan succeeded, more or less, despite repeated rebellions and even the temporary relocation of the court to other cities by some of his successors.

Two dynasties actually shaped the city. While Isabel I of Castile and Fernando II of Aragon were the first monarchs to unite the 15 kingdoms into a loose confederation, they spent most of their efforts forcing the Moors back to North Africa and consolidating their rule. Given the profound events of 1492 and their repercussions, the monarchs didn't spend much time in the future capital. It was their great-grandson, Felipe II, who declared Madrid the capital of what was then—1561—the largest empire in the world. He was the second of a succession of Hapsburgs to rule the troubled empire, and one of his first acts was to commission the architect Juan de Herrera to design the Plaza Mayor. His descendants and the monarchs of the subsequent Bourbon dynasty were responsible for shaping what comprises the heart and soul of the city.

Actually few attempts have been made to achieve grandeur in Madrid, at least in comparison with Paris and London. But the city does enjoy a magnificent palace; several major east-west boulevards; world-renowned art collections at the Prado as well as at several smaller museums and convents; and three large parks that provide beauty and open space.

Most of the Hapsburg and Bourbon contributions to the city are located near the east-west Calle de Alcalá and its western extension—the Calle del Arenal. What remains of medieval Madrid is situated south of the Calle Mayor and the Plaza Mayor. The following walk encompasses both the royal and plebian sections of the old city.

● ● ● ● ● ● ● ● ● ● ● ● ● ● ● ●

Start on the north side of:

1. **Puerta del Sol** (Gate of the Sun). There may have been a gate here, perhaps when the first city wall was erected in the 13th century. The name is at least symbolic, since 10 streets converge in this half-moon-shaped plaza. It is known as "kilometer zero" since this is the point from which all

La Ciudad Antigua

9993

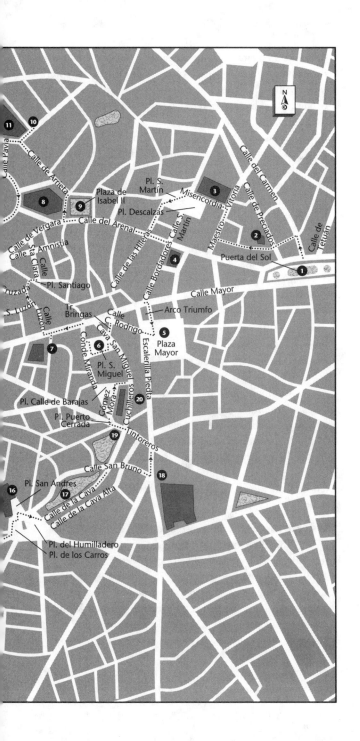

distances on major roads are measured as they fan out across the central region of Castile. Once, the sidewalks here were filled with café tables, but now these cafés have generally been replaced by fast-food restaurants. The trolley cars that used to fill this area are also gone, and much of the space is now used as bays for buses; the metro station under the plaza has been renovated and enlarged. During the last decade, the buildings in the area have been spiffed up, most of the larger advertising signs removed, and a couple of fountains installed. Despite these renovations, the Puerta del Sol has few attractions except for access to transportation elsewhere. Since the old city of the Hapsburgs and Bourbons lies to the west and south, this is a logical place to begin your exploration.

To orient yourself, stand behind the equestrian statue of Carlos III at the "top" of the rounded side of the plaza. This Carlos was an enlightened monarch in the context of his time (late 18th century) and deserves much credit for transforming Madrid from a slovenly backwater town into a respectable capital during his reign. The Palacio Real became his residence, and he is responsible for the erection of many other prominent buildings and monuments.

Turn around so that you face north and look at the statue of a bear nibbling a tree. This is the symbol of the city of Madrid. The tree, which is called *madroño,* produces a fruit similar to strawberries. Walk past the bear and enter the largely pedestrian shopping district. At the next corner, turn left on Calle de Tetuán. Continue past the entrance of the main branch of:

2. **El Corte Inglés,** Spain's most prominent department store chain. The name means, in this case, "The English Cut," referring to tailoring, not "The English Court." Owing to a 1980s policy change, the store remains open during the customary three-hour afternoon siesta period. That dramatic attempt to align Spain with the customs of other Western nations hasn't persuaded many retailers to change their ways, but it's nice to know that this store is open all afternoon.

Two blocks later, turn right on Calle Maestro Vitoria, then take the next left on Calle Misericordia. This street quickly widens into a small plaza in front of the:

3. **Monasterio-Museo de las Descalzas Reales,** a Renaissance palace that was transformed into a convent in 1559 by Juana de Austria, daughter of Carlos V, the Holy Roman Emperor. She became a nun there after its conversion. The children of royalty and the well-to-do came to the convent for their schooling. Many lived here until their parents eventually arranged marriages for them elsewhere in Europe. The convent is sumptuously furnished with paintings by such artists as Zurbarán, Titian, and Rubens; Flemish tapestries depicting cartoons by Rubens; and almost three dozen chapels filled with gold and silver ornamentation. Although the guided tour moves through the convent rather quickly and offers commentary in Spanish only, a visit is worthwhile. The visiting hours are short, since this is still a functioning convent, and they are subject to change. As of early 1995 the convent was open from 10:30am to 12:30pm and 4 to 5:30pm Tuesday through Thursday and Saturday; 10:30am to 12:30pm Friday; and 11am to 1:30pm on Sunday.

As you exit the monastery, turn right. Walk across the Plaza San Martin and turn left down the Calle de la Hileras. Turn left on Calle del Arenal (which means "sandpit"). The street covers what used to be a stream. Cross over and, after 1 block, turn right on Calle Bordadores. Immediately on the left is the:

4. **Iglesia de San Ginés,** which stands on the site of an early Christian church that may have dated back to the period of Moorish rule (10th century). The present building dates from the mid-17th century. Among the works of art inside is El Greco's painting of Christ expelling the moneychangers.

At the top of the hill is Calle Mayor; on the other side you can see an opening in the phalanx of buildings. Cross over and go up that alley, which leads into the:

5. **Plaza Mayor,** one of the great public spaces in Spain. To get the best perspective, walk to the equestrian statue of Felipe III at the center. Although not as ambitious or intellectual as his father, Felipe III deserves the credit for this grand plaza. He died in 1621, just two years after its completion.

The rectangular plaza is surrounded by apartment and office buildings with balustraded windows, all a terracotta color and uniform height except for the twin conical turrets on either side of the Casa Panadería. Formerly a municipal bakery, it can easily be identified by the somewhat amateurish murals that were added a few years ago. Royalty preferred its balconies for watching both joyous and gruesome events—mass executions, bullfights, and *autos-da-fé* (the torturing of heretics and criminals)—in the plaza below. Now, traffic is banned and the square is for pedestrians only; café tables extend out toward Felipe III from three sides. The restaurants and bars that own the tables are tucked away behind the ground-floor arcade that runs all the way around the plaza. The food here is not memorable and the drinks are expensive, but it is a delightful place to stop for a while.

There is much of interest to see here. Caricaturists set up shop near the tables, musicians stroll, women sell flowers, young people flirt, and everyone promenades. Throughout the summer, and especially during the city-wide Fiesta de San Isidro in May, the plaza fills up almost nightly for rock concerts and performances of the light opera called *zarzuela,* for fireworks, and for ceremonial formations of horsemen in 18th-century garb.

To continue your walk, face the Panadería for orientation. It's on the north side of the plaza. Walk over to the portal at the northwest corner and exit. On the other side, down to your left, is the:

6. **Mercado de San Miguel,** the glass-covered central market. Walk down and enter at the closest door. The tidy booths and counters inside are paeans to the bounty of the Spanish countryside and to the Spanish fishing fleet, Europe's largest. Produce is heaped in a voluptuous profusion of shining melons, glistening grapes, and dewy greens; whole hams hang in rows from their hooves next to curtains of sausages; all manner of shellfish and crustaceans are splayed across beds of shaved ice. The best time to see the market is in the early morning hours, when the stocks are full; however, the aromas and sights are nearly as vivid several hours later, just before the lunchtime closing.

Castizos and Madrileños

Since foreign visitors first started writing their observations, they have criticized Madrid as being the least "Spanish" of Spain's cities. They alleged that Madrileños adapted themselves too eagerly to outside customs and fashions, while ignoring their own distinctive Spanish traditions. Barcelona dances its *sardana,* Seville has *sevillanas,* Zaragosa whirls to the *jota,* and Galicia resounds to the wail of its bagpipe, the *gaita.* The critics ask, "What is distinctive about Madrid? Where is its folk culture?"

Ask the *castizos.* That is what ordinary people call themselves. *Castizo* has several interrelated meanings: pure, authentic, well-bred, prolific, all pertaining to the chest-thumping pride of working-class Madrileños. *Castizo* is also a dialect derived from standard Castilian Spanish. The *castizos* also have their *chotis*—a dance performed within a small imaginary square, with a man and woman facing each other, their backs straight, feet together, and hips moving in a way that could be described as a Victorian antecedent of the Twist. Some of the dancers wear native costumes. A subgroup called *chulos* may dress up on special occasions. The men wear snug Edwardian coats and trousers and billowing cravats. Some *chulos* have recently sewn buttons all over their suits. The woman (*chulas*) wear polka-dot or flowered dresses that fall in tiered flounces to the ankle, with shawls over their heads and carnations in their hair.

Thus decked out, *chulos* often parade in the Plaza Mayor, especially during such events as the Festival of San Isidro in May. They may also appear at *verbenas*—neighborhood fiestas seldom seen by tourists. And they frequently portray characters in a *zarzuela*—a distinct Castilian form of operetta with its own theater in Madrid, the **Teatro de la Zarzuela** (Calle Principe 25, tel. 429-6297).

After a tour, exit via the main door and turn left. Within a few steps, you will reach an open space on the right—the small Plaza de San Miguel. Cross the plaza to the other side and turn left. You will be once again on Calle Mayor. Stay on this side. One block down Calle Mayor, on the left, is the:

7. **Plaza de la Villa,** one of Madrid's oldest group of buildings dating from the Hapsburg era (16th–17th centuries). In the center is a statue of Admiral Alvaro de Bazán, hero of a memorable victory at sea, when Spain and its allies defeated the Turks at Lepanto (1571). More than 33,000 men died in that single naval battle, which gave Christian nations hegemony over the Mediterranean. Among the thousands of sailors wounded was Miguel de Cervantes, author of *Don Quijote.*

Entering the plaza, you will see the tower on the left—the Torre de los Lujánes. It was built in the Mudejar style, favored by Moorish artisans who lived under Catholic rule. Although it employs characteristic Mudejar brick patterns alternating with bands of cement and rubble, there is also a late Gothic doorway, finished in 1494. It is believed that the French king François I, taken prisoner in the battle of Pavía in 1525, may have spent part of his confinement here. If so, he wasn't deterred by the experience, since he later waged three more wars against Carlos V.

Next on the left is the **Hemeroteca,** with Gothic and Renaissance elements inside the front door. Continuing in clockwise fashion, you will see the **Casa de Cisneros,** the building at the back of the plaza that was completed in the mid-16th century. A second-story bridge connects the Casa de Cisneros with the old town hall, which dates from the same period and is now called the **Casa de la Villa.**

Opposite the open end of the plaza is a narrow street called Calle Señores de Luzón. Cross Calle Mayor and enter that street, which will take you to the Plaza de Santiago, with a church on the far side. Walk to the right, passing in front of the church, and turn left on Calle de Santa Clara. After 1 block, this street will bring you to Plaza de Ramales. At the corner of Calle Amnistía is:

Take a Break Café Las Asturias, Plaza de Ramales s/n (tel. 248-7554). This café with its marble-topped tables attracts a large number of students and professors. The bar at the back displays cakes and tarts under glass, and the menu lists a variety of sandwiches, canapés, and drinks. Each drink is served with a dish of dried fruit and nuts. The café is usually open from noon to 3am, but the hours vary.

As you leave the café, turn right, then right again at the next corner, into Calle de Vergara. At the foot of this street is the:

8. **Teatro Real,** traditionally the primary venue for opera and classical music. In recent years, however, it has been embraced in scaffolding, swathed in canvas, and bristling with construction cranes. Attempts at renovation have been hampered by the fact that the metro trains rumble beneath the theater, disturbing performances and threatening the structural integrity of the building.

Turn right and cross the street. Behind the theater is the park called:

9. **Plaza de Isabel II,** which has also been undergoing renovation. If possible, cut across the plaza immediately behind the theater and turn left on Calle de Arrieta. If construction blocks your way, continue to the far end of the park, where there is a statue of Isabel II, and turn left on Arrieta. Follow that street as it branches away from the north side of the theater. This street will soon bring you to the Plaza de la Encarnación. On the right, at number 2 is:

10. **Alambique,** one of the first stores in Spain to stock a large variety of gourmet cookware and related gadgets. It also offers classes in several Spanish regional cuisines and techniques (some of which are taught in English). The store is open Monday through Saturday.

Directly ahead, across a patch of lawn, is the:

11. **Monasterio-Museo de la Encarnación.** The statue in front is of the poet and playwright Félix Lope de Vega Carpio, who founded the Spanish dramatic theater and wrote almost 1,800 plays. Despite his numerous love

affairs, he was active in the church and assumed a number of prominent religious positions in his later years (the early 18th century, during the reign of Felipe III and construction of this monastery).

The principal attraction of this monastery is a lavishly outfitted Baroque room housing some 1,500 relics of little-known saints. The monastery is open Wednesday and Saturday from 10:30 to 11:30am and 4 to 5:30pm, and Sunday from 11am to 1:30pm.

Keep to the left of the monastery and to the left of the Jardines del Cabo Noval, a pocket park next to the Calle Pavía. Through the trees, up ahead and to the right, you can see the Palacio Real. Follow the curving street around the:

12. **Plaza de Oriente;** on your left you will see the Teatro Real. In the center of the plaza is yet another equestrian statue—of Felipe IV. When he commissioned Pietro de Tacca to create the statue, he ordered that his horse be sculpted rearing up on his hind legs. Initially perplexed, the sculptor wondered how to support the entire heavy statue on only two legs. He solved the problem by hollowing out the front half of the statue and making the back solid. The statue is adorned at its base with a cascade fountain and lion sculptures. The plaza itself has numerous trees, flower plots, and knee-level topiary. Felipe IV is perhaps best remembered as a patron of the great Renaissance painter, Velázquez, who produced many portraits of the royal family.

Continue to the end of this street, which curves around the plaza, and you will reach the:

Take a Break Café de Oriente, Plaza de Oriente 2 (tel. 541-3974 or 547-1564). A pragmatic priest named Luis Lezama opened his first restaurant to help teach ex-convicts and troubled boys a profession. That restaurant soon became a chain, with branches in Seville, the Costa del Sol, and now, Washington, D.C. This one was his second restaurant, and it remains enormously popular, with its tables outdoors in nice weather, its fin-de-siècle interior, and velvet banquettes lining the front. Several specialty coffees are available to accompany the pastries displayed on the bar; *tapas* and other snacks are also offered. Open daily from late morning until after midnight.

From the café, walk along the south side of the plaza toward the palace. Statues depicting Visigoth and Roman notables have lined this side of the plaza ever since it was discovered they were too heavy for the roofline railing of the palace. Use the crosswalk to cross the busy Calle de Bailen and turn left to the:

13. **Palacio Real.** The second most popular attraction in Madrid (after the Prado Museum), the neoclassical Royal Palace has an almost unimaginable 2,000 rooms, more than three times the number in Buckingham Palace. Carlos III was the first monarch to live there (1764). The present king and queen, Juan Carlos and Sofía, use it only for occasional state ceremonies; they prefer to live at a much smaller residence (Zarzuela) in the suburbs. At the end of the palace wall, turn right. You will soon reach the visitors' entrance to the palace. Guided tours are available in several languages. In the reception area at the far end of the courtyard, visitors assemble by language group until there are enough people to justify a tour. This rarely takes longer than 30 minutes, and the tour itself is about an hour.

Only about 50 of the palace's salons and chambers are open to visitors, depending upon ongoing renovations, but that sample is enough to overwhelm the senses. Perhaps only Versailles could surpass this palace in opulence. One of the stunning rooms usually included on the tour is the main dining room with a table that can accommodate 145 diners; there is gold-rimmed stemware and porcelain so fine that the shadow of one's hand can be seen through it. Guests dine beneath the glitter of 15 massive crystal chandeliers. Many rooms are hung with priceless Flemish and Castilian tapestries as well as large royal portraits by such notables as Goya and El Greco.

Back in the courtyard, to the left of the entrance, is the royal armory, with walls of weapons and countless suits of armor for both men and horses, the helmets plumed and the breastplates gleaming. There are even wee metal outfits in which the royal children clanked about.

The building opposite the south end of the palace is:

14. **Nuestra Señora de la Almudena.** Begun in the late 19th century, it is slated to become the official cathedral of Madrid, which inexplicably doesn't have one. This structure will not be completed for many years, though. At the end of the windblown plaza that separates the palace from the future cathedral is another statue of Felipe III (see Stop no. 5). If you stand on the statue's platform, you will have a nice view of the Campo del Moro, a park immediately below the palace; the Manzanares River that borders it; and the Casa de Campo, a large, semiwild preserve that was formerly a royal hunting ground. During the siege of Madrid in the Civil War of 1936–39, the Nationalist artillery batteries were positioned in the park, loosing daily barrages on the Loyalist defenders of the city at the front line in University City, about a mile north of the the palace. Now, on clear days, one can glimpse the palace-monastery of Felipe II—El Escorial—on the horizon.

Turn around and return between the palace and unfinished cathedral to the Calle Bailen, turning right. Over on the left-hand side of Bailen is one of Madrid's oldest taverns, **El Anciano Rey de los Vinos.** If there's a pause in the rush of traffic, you might want to make a detour and look inside while enjoying a glass of draft cider *(sidra)*. Otherwise, continue on this side of the street, which soon crosses a 19th-century viaduct high over the Calle de Segovia. That street used to be an arroyo, often filled with water, that ran down to the Manzanares. Far below, to the right, are sparse ruins of fortifications that protected the Moorish settlement of Mayrit more than 1,000 years ago. The viaduct has attracted a fair number of suicidal Madrileños ever since it was completed.

At the far end of the viaduct, on the right, is:

Take a Break El Ventorillo, Bailen 14. This is an ideal spot for looking out over the Casa de Campo and catching a glimpse of the Sierra de Guadarrama. The tables are set out every year on April 23rd, the day Cervantes died. For the price of one or two drinks, one can secure a table; the food available is not exceptional. Open daily.

Papa Does Battle

After the success of his novel *The Sun Also Rises,* which was set primarily in Spain, Ernest Hemingway gave up journalism to devote himself to writing fiction. However, the outbreak of the Spanish Civil War drew him back to his earlier profession, with a contract that paid him nearly a dollar a word for his news dispatches—a princely sum at that time. Hemingway entered Madrid in March 1937 from the east (the city was under siege from the west) and sped down the Gran Via to the seedy Hotel Florida, which stood on the Plaza de Callao. There were daily bombardments and trench warfare in the University City district, about 20 blocks up the Calle de la Princesa, the extension of Gran Via.

Papa's journalism wasn't tainted by bland objectivity. He was firmly on the side of the Loyalists and against what he called "the fascist Italian German Moorish invasion" led by Franco. While filing his dispatches, Hemingway was discussing plans to make a propaganda film, *The Spanish Earth,* to support the Loyalist cause. Among those who planned to work with him on the film were Lillian Hellman and John Dos Passos. "Dos" was in Madrid at the same time as "Hem."

Ernest was at the top of his form at that time. "Difficulty and danger were elements in which he flourished," wrote his biographer, Carlos Baker, and "this was the kind of experience by which he could grow, adding new dimensions to his stature as a novelist." There were occasional diversions in battered Madrid. One day, a Rebel shell made a direct hit on the hot water tank at the hotel. Steam billowed through the halls, forcing the guests out of their rooms. Many unsuspected liaisons were thus revealed. Ernest and another writer, Martha Gellhorn, emerged from his room. He was married, but to another woman. However, Martha became his wife in 1940, the same year that *For Whom the Bell Tolls* was published. Papa had a habit of marrying his girlfriends.

Continue down Calle de Bailen; after 3 blocks you will reach the:

15. **Iglesia de San Francisco el Grande,** to the right of the traffic circle. Designed an 18th-century neoclassical style with a bowed front and a large central dome, its chapels have paintings by Goya and Zurbarán. The church is usually open just during mass.

Turn left from Calle de Bailen and walk up Carrera San Francisco, which has less traffic and is somewhat quieter than Bailen. After 3 blocks, to the left of the Plaza Puerta de Moros (Gate of the Moors) is the:

16. **Capilla del Obispo,** the 16th-century "Bishop's Chapel." One of the oldest churches in Madrid, it's been undergoing restoration for some time, and the reopening date is not certain. Stolidly Gothic outside, the interior has some exuberant Plateresque elements and a complex and adroitly carved retable, which is worth seeing if possible.

Otherwise, continue through the Plaza Puerta de Moros, which merges with the Plaza del Humilladero on the left. Actually, these "plazas" are of little interest since they are simply street intersections. So cross over to:

17. **Calle de la Cava Baja,** which is slightly to the left of Calle de la Cava Alta. It has been constructed along the edge of a former moat that protected 12th-century fortifications. For decades (perhaps even centuries) this narrow byway has been lined with taverns. In earlier times, they were probably frequented by farmers and rural people who came to town to sell their goods; now many of these establishments cater to the well-to-do. On the right, for example, is the deceptively humble-looking Casa Lucio at number 35; popular for its traditional Castilian food, including succulent roast lamb and suckling pig, it now attracts government ministers, members of the royal family, and top-level businesspeople. Reservations are usually required. A few doors farther along, at number 27, La Soleá is a cramped two-room bar that caters to homesick Andalucians who squeeze in every night to hear flamenco *canto,* the soul music of their native region in southern Spain. They demonstrate their enthusiasm for the

several singers who pour out laments for lost love and missed opportunity.

One long block later, there is an opening on the right, next to El Schotis restaurant, called Calle San Bruno. Take that, as well as the slight jog to the left, and you will emerge onto Calle de Toledo. Across the street is the:

18. **Cathedral San Isidro el Real.** Actually, its status as Madrid's cathedral is only temporary—just until Nuestra Señora de la Almudena opens officially. Unfortunately, the interior of this building is not too interesting; it was ravaged during the Civil War and no attempt has been made to replace the stolen artwork and other treasures.

Turn left along Calle de Toledo and then left on Calle de Tintoreros. You will soon arrive at the:

19. **Plaza de Puerta Cerrada** (Closed Door). Another gate of the 12th-century city walls was here, although no remnant is left. In the middle of the plaza is a marble cross on a pedestal. Many of Madrid's city squares once had such crosses, but all except this one were removed during the frenzied antireligious hysteria of the early 1930s. The houses that face this plaza have painted murals on their sides depicting an abundance of meat, fish, fruits, and vegetables to commemorate the markets that were once located in this area. Staying on the right, cross Calle de los Cuchillieros. Soon you will come to the glossy crimson, green, and brown facade of:

Take a Break   Casa Paco, Plaza Puerta Cerrada 11 (tel. 366-3166). This historic *taberna* founded in 1870 has no seats in the front room. The handsomely carved bar is surrounded by a high dado of colorful tiles. A period poster commemorates the notable 1947 confrontation at Madrid's *plaza de toros* between the legendary matadors Manolete and Dominguin. The preferred beverage here is Valdepeñas wine poured from unlabeled carafes into eggcup-sized tumblers. Just ask for *tinto* or *blanco.* There is no beer and no coffee machine. The only food in the front room is a few simple *tapas.* Yet Casa Paco has hosted King Juan Carlos, a former U.S. president, and a clutch of Hollywood stars. A dining room in back serves traditional meals.

As you leave Casa Paco, turn right, and right again at the corner of the tavern into Calle Gómez de Mora. This leads into the quiet Plaza del Conde de Barajas. Proceed straight ahead and turn right on Calle del Maestro Villa. This ends at Calle de Cuchilleros ("Street of the Cutlers") named for the former shops of cutlery merchants that used to line this curving street. Now, the street is filled with restaurants and taverns. The best known by far is down on the right, on the opposite side. Nearly as obligatory as a stop as the Prado Museum is:

20. **Botín,** 17 Calle de Cuchilleros, perhaps the oldest restaurant in Madrid—dating back to 1725. The atmospheric cellar as well as the four floors above are packed with antiques, tiles, and memorabilia. It would require many visits to be able to observe all the details. Despite the large crowds that dine here daily, greetings by the staff are uncommonly cordial. The food is traditional Castilian, featuring hearty portions of roasts. There is no bar, and reservations for meals are usually necessary. Some of the action in Hemingway's novel *The Sun Also Rises* was set here when Lady Brett brushed off Jake Barnes.

Turn around and retrace your steps up the street toward the flight of stairs that ascends up through the Arco de Cuchilleros into the Plaza Mayor. Near the foot of the stairs is another restaurant, El Cuchi, whose awning informs English-speaking visitors that "Hemingway Never Ate Here."

Castizo and Cultural Madrid

Start: Puerta del Sol (Metro: Sol).

Finish: Plaza de la Cibeles.

Time: 3 to 4 hours, not including rest stops.

Best Times: Any day from 9am to 1pm and 4 to 7pm April through October, 9am to 3pm November through March.

Worst Times: August; siesta periods (usually 1:30 to 5pm), when most shops and other sites are closed; winter evenings after 5pm.

Spain's vaunted Golden Age coincided with the peak and decline of its Empire of Two Worlds; it was fueled by the pillaged treasures of American Indians and fired by the religious and territorial conflicts that accompanied the Renaissance. The painters Velázquez, El Greco, Murillo, Zurbarán and Ribera; playwrights Lope de Vega and Calderón de la Barca; and poet-novelist Miguel Cervantes were all active from the middle or late 16th century into the 17th, a period of scarcely three generations. Nearly all the poets,

Castizo and Cultural Madrid

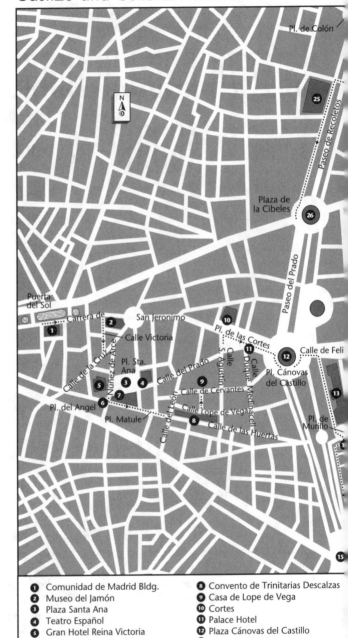

1. Comunidad de Madrid Bldg.
2. Museo del Jamón
3. Plaza Santa Ana
4. Teatro Español
5. Gran Hotel Reina Victoria
6. Plaza del Angel
7. Calle de las Huertas
8. Convento de Trinitarias Descalzas
9. Casa de Lope de Vega
10. Cortes
11. Palace Hotel
12. Plaza Cánovas del Castillo
13. Museo del Prado
14. Jardín Botánico

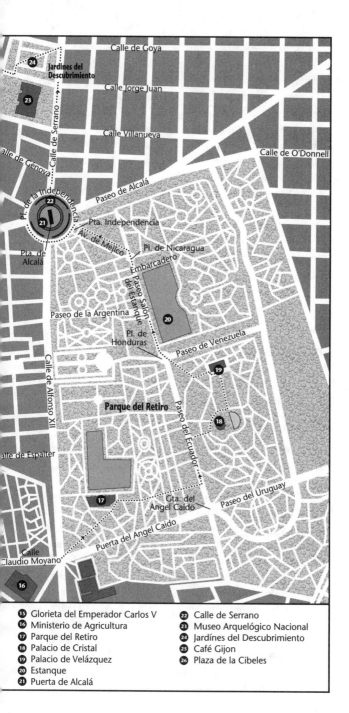

Calle de Goya

Jardines del Descubrimiento

Calle Jorge Juan

Calle Villanueva

Calle de O'Donnell

Calle de Génova

Calle de Serrano

Paseo de Alcalá

Pl. de la Independencia

Pta. Independencia

Pta. de Alcalá

Av. de Méjico

Pl. de Nicaragua

Embarcadero

Paseo Salón del Estanque

Paseo de la Argentina

Pl. de Honduras

Paseo de Venezuela

Calle de Alfonso XII

Parque del Retiro

Paseo del Ecuador

Calle de Espalter

Gta. del Angel Caído

Paseo del Uruguay

Puerta del Angel Caído

Calle Claudio Moyano

🕒 Glorieta del Emperador Carlos V
🕕 Ministerio de Agricultura
🕗 Parque del Retiro
🕘 Palacio de Cristal
🕙 Palacio de Velázquez
🕛 Estanque
🕐 Puerta de Alcalá

🕝 Calle de Serrano
🕞 Museo Arquelógico Nacional
🕟 Jardínes del Descubrimiento
🕠 Café Gijon
🕡 Plaza de la Cibeles

dramatists, and novelists of that era lived and worked in the *barrios* to the south and southeast of the Puerta del Sol. These labyrinthine streets were the locus of Madrid's literary and theatrical scene at the time and, to a degree, still are. This section is also the home of working-class people—*castizos.* This confluence of cultures gives the Plaza Santa Ana neighborhood a particular verve and piquancy, especially since there are also numerous *tapas* bars (known as *tascas* or *mesónes*) as well as music clubs and drinking spots ("bars of the night").

East of this district, the Paseo del Prado connects four of Madrid's most important museums. There are also the lakes and gardens of the 300-acre Retiro Park and the shopping streets of upscale Salamanca. This walk connects the city of Cervantes with the Madrid of today.

• • • • • • • • • • • • • • • •

Start on the south side of the Puerta del Sol, in front of the:

1. **Comunidad de Madrid Building** (the one with the clock tower). On New Year's Eve, Madrileños by the thousands pour into this plaza. They come supplied with grapes, and when the hands of the clock reach midnight, everyone in the plaza pops a grape into his or her mouth at each of the twelve chimes. Imbedded in the sidewalk in front of the building is a plaque identifying that spot as "kilometer zero," from which all distances in Spain are presumably measured.

   This plaza has a bloody history. After a popular uprising on May 2, 1808, against the French troops who were occupying the city, scores of Madrileños were summarily executed here. That event was the subject of some of Francisco Goya's most famous paintings, and the date *Dos de Mayo* reverberates as strongly in the Spanish psyche as July 4th does for Americans. The building here was also used for deplorable purposes during the 36 years of Franco's rule; it was the central police headquarters. The screams of prisoners under interrogation were regularly heard, and many of their deaths were reported as "suicides." This building now houses the offices of the recently created autonomous federal district of Madrid.

Tapa to *Tapa* to *Tapa*

Food guru Craig Claiborne called *tapas* "one of the greatest culinary inventions of all time." Although the origin of this dish is unknown, several conjectures have been advanced.

One holds that back before Madrid had hotels and restaurants as we now know them, there were hostelries where one could raise a tankard, gnaw on a joint of meat, and spend the night on a bed of straw (usually in the company of strangers). Madrid was a notoriously filthy city, since it was filled with domesticated animals, and residents habitually tossed garbage and human waste into the streets.

Such domestic practices resulted in swarms of insects. A clever innkeeper may have noticed the flies buzzing around his customers and their drinks and attempted to alleviate the problem by covering the wine goblets with slices of bread. (*Tapa* means "lid" or "cover.") Perhaps another tavern owner heard about this and also tried it. Soon, everyone was doing it. Then, perhaps someone wanted to distinguish his bread from everyone else's by putting a piece of cheese on top. Later, someone else thought of adding ham to the cheese. In no time, the lids were being piled with anchovies, liver bits, eggs, or whatever was available. The battle for the hearts and stomachs of Madrileños escalated. Eventually, leaf-sized dishes of nuts, olives, chicken wings, shrimp, or whatever were routinely served with, not on, tumblers of wine.

Whatever the origin of *tapas*, there are now at least 3,000 tascas or mesónes in Madrid. A restaurant typically has a *tapas* bar in the front room and a dining room at the rear or upstairs. The counter itself may be crowded with platters of prepared or raw foods, or there may be a written menu indicating what is available. Up to 60 items may be offered. Two people often begin by sharing several *tapas* and then ordering more depending upon their appetite. *Tapas* are portions served in saucers, while *raciónes* are two or three times larger, and one or two might be adequate for a light meal.

Face the center of the plaza (north). Walk east (to the right) and you will enter the Carrera de San Jeronimo, one of the 10 streets that meet here. One block after leaving the Puerta del Sol, turn right on Calle Victoria. At that corner is a *tapas* bar and restaurant called the:

2. **Museo del Jamón** (Museum of Ham). Ham is Spain's favorite meat, and this *museo* is lined on three sides with countless whole hog legs nudging each other like bowling pins in a barrel. They are hung by their ankles and still-attached cloven hooves. Conical cups beneath each ham catch vagrant drops of fat. The hams are air-cured, as a rule, but in a variety of ways. It is claimed that one type is buried each winter in the snows of the Sierra Nevada and dug up in the spring. The hams are usually identified by their area of origin; Teruel and Jabugo are among the most prized and most expensive (3 ounces of the best can cost more than $20).

The Museum of Ham is an appropriate introduction to a *barrio* that has few monuments but brims with life. Go up Calle Victoria, which is lined with restaurants and taverns. The windows along here display more edible exotica than most North Americans have ever seen before. Certainly there are lots of shrimp *(gambas)* fanned out across beds of ice, in surprisingly varied sizes and configurations *(langostinos, gambones, cigalas),* and what appear to be fried onion rings but are actually squid *(calamares).* But in season you may also see razor clams *(navajas)* shaped like fat pencils, sea snails *(caracoles del mar)* in pretty spiky shells, earthenware dishes of beansprout-like baby eels *(angulas),* and thumb-sized barnacles *(percebes)* with horny hooves and crinkled black flesh. Most of these are increasingly rare delicacies and predictably expensive but cost far less than Maine lobster *(bogavente),* which may go for the equivalent of $50 or more.

A meal consisting of *tapas* can be filling, enormously satisfying, *and* economical. Since every tavern along this route is likely to have a menu posted outside, you can easily avoid costly errors.

Calle Victoria is known for more than intriguing aromas and countless Madrileños and tourists consuming platters of food. It is also the locus of bullfighting publicity, with posters announcing upcoming *corridas* and enterprising ticket-sellers looking for prospective buyers. Owing to the higher prices asked by these entrepreneurs, it would be better to buy your tickets from an established ticket agency or ask your hotel concierge to get them for you. The usual commission is about 20% (it will be higher if there are headliner matadors or if the bullfight is scheduled during the May Festival of San Isidro).

Turn left on Calle de la Cruz, then immediately right on Calle Núñez de Arce. Soon, on the right, you will see:

☕ Take a Break La Trucha, Núñez de Arce 6 (tel. 532-0882). Although there are many *tabernas* to choose from in this area, this one provides an exceptionally friendly welcome. The house specialty here is *verbenas,* which means "festivals" but refers to a tantalizing plate of smoked fish and inky roe. Many other *tapas* are also available, most of which are prepared to order. La Trucha is open Monday through Saturday from noon to midnight.

Continue on Núñez de Arce to the:

3. **Plaza Santa Ana.** Here on the corner you will see a building covered with ambitious tile murals. Called the Villa Rosa, it has housed a flamenco *tablao,* a private club, and, more recently, a disco. The plaza, which slopes down to the left, has been subject to many renovation efforts, but none has entirely succeeded. The plaza is simply too popular, in constant use by children, families, street people, theatergoers, and *tapas* crawlers. Two sides are lined with bars and restaurants, including, on the south side, **La Moderna, Naturbier,** and **Cervecería Alemaña** (a Hemingway favorite), and on the north, **Viña P** and **Platerías.** At the lower end of the plaza is the:

4. **Teatro Español,** which borders the Calle del Principe— a center of Madrid's vigorous theatrical scene since the 16th century. In the earliest times, plays (mostly comedies) were staged in arenas open to the sky. These were boisterous events, with heavy drinking, catcalls, and frequent brawls among those sitting in the least expensive seats. With the construction of enclosed buildings, the audience became more polite and orderly. Since 1869

this theater has produced comedies and dramas by Spain's greatest playwrights, including Félix Lope de Vega, José de Echegaray, Lope de Rueda, Federico García Lorca, and Pedro Calderón de la Barca. (The statue at this end of the park is of Calderón.)

Continue clockwise around the plaza. At the next corner is the:

5. **Gran Hotel Reina Victoria,** which was extensively upgraded in the late 1980s into a four-star, first-class hotel. It may seem rather elegant for the neighborhood now, but it still hints of its past as a favorite gathering place for toreros, promoters, and hangers-on in the bullfighting business. The revered Manolete often stayed here, and the area appealed to Hemingway.

Bordering the hotel on the other side is:

6. **Plaza del Angel,** a cramped triangular space, noted primarily because one of Madrid's top music emporiums, Café Central, is at number 10. High-quality live jazz is the usual attraction, but the management also presents folksingers, Latin salsa, or blues.

At the next corner, turn left on:

7. **Calle de las Huertas.** A less prepossessing street would be difficult to imagine, at least during the day, when it is dark and shuttered. Come back at night, though, and it blazes with activity when some 50 neighborhood bars and cafés throw open their doors. There are conventional *tascas;* Irish pubs; dance clubs; and bars specializing in whatever drinks or foods are currently in fashion. Hundreds (perhaps thousands) of patrons keep the energy level high and the cash registers busy until the wee hours. If you would like to return later for the evening's festivities, take note of **Casa Alberto** (number 18), an atmospheric tavern on the ground floor of a house where Cervantes once lived; **Café Jazz Populart** (number 22), which showcases jazz combos and blues groups as well as Afro-Caribbean performers; and **Muñiz** (number 29), a bar known for its countless varieties of *tapas,* if not its decor.

Continue down Huertas for 3 blocks and turn left on Calle de León; after 1 block, turn right on Calle Lope de Vega. On the right you will see a long brick building, the:

8. **Convento de Trinitarias Descalzas.** At about the midway point along the wall is a large stone plaque, skillfully carved in neoclassical style. Bearing a relief profile of a man with a ruffed collar, it announces that Miguel de Cervantes Saavedra is buried there. He died in a house around the corner in 1616 shortly after completing the second half of his immortal *Don Quijote.* The convent is still home to cloistered nuns who shun almost all contact with the outside world.

Turn left at the next corner, the Calle de San Agustín, then left again on Calle de Cervantes. About 20 yards ahead on the right is the:

9. **Casa de Lope de Vega,** home of the prominent playwright and contemporary of Cervantes. Although their relationship was at first friendly, they eventually became bitter rivals because of some enmity on the part of Lope. So it is somewhat ironic that Lope died on a street named Cervantes, while the novelist is buried on Calle Lope de Vega. Astonishingly prolific, the poet and dramatist wrote about 1,800 plays during his lifetime (1562–1635), beginning at the age of 12. By all reports, he was equally relentless in pursuing countless romantic liaisons, leading some analysts to wonder whether he suffered from what would later be diagnosed as satyriasis.

Lope de Vega lived from 1610 until his death in this somewhat modest house, which was recently renovated and furnished as it would have been in his lifetime. The house is open to visitors Monday through Friday from 9:30am to 3pm and Saturdays from 10am to 2pm.

Retrace your steps back down Calle de Cervantes. At the intersection of Calle San Agustín is:

Take a Break Sixto Gran Mesón, Cervantes 28 (tel. 429-2255). At street level there is a long bar laden with earthenware platters of food. Use of ceramic tiles and overhead dark wooden beams provide a pleasant Castilian setting that is more inviting than many rough-and-tumble *tapas* bars. Thus, this establishment tends to attract families with children. The pricey specialty is seafood salad. Upstairs is a formal dining room, with a working fireplace that is especially appreciated on blustery days. Open daily

Candide of La Mancha

Miguel de Cervantes Saavedra's own life was far more epic and fraught with peril than that of his fictional hero, Don Quijote. Cervantes was born in Alcalá de Henares, a university town east of Madrid. In 1569 he went to Italy, possibly to escape conviction for an illegal swordfight. For about a year, he studied philosophy and literature while serving a cardinal. He then enlisted in the Spanish army and participated in the naval battle of Lepanto, in which Spain and its allies achieved a great victory over the Turks. After additional military service, Cervantes set off for Spain in 1575. His ship was waylaid and he was captured by Barbary pirates, who sold him into slavery in Algiers. He remained a slave until his family ransomed him five years later. He returned to Madrid, but the ransom had bankrupted his family. While seeking regular employment, he began to write and completed a novel and more than 20 plays. In 1588 Cervantes obtained a government position in Seville as a naval purchasing agent. Not adept at finance, he ran up a series of deficits over the next nine years that resulted in several short prison terms.

Broke again and out of work, Cervantes all but "disappeared" in 1597. He reemerged in 1604 with the completed first half of *Don Quijote de la Mancha*, some of it probably written during his final jail term. It was an immediate success. Rather than continue writing the second half of the novel, Cervantes tried to return to the theater. His new fame as a novelist didn't help, possibly due to the machinations of Lope de Vega, who wanted to protect his own status as the nation's foremost dramatist. A spurious second half of *Quijote* was published in 1614 under the pseudonym of Avellanade. Cervantes was thus compelled to write his own triumphant version, published in 1615—less than a year before his death.

Don Quijote was eventually translated into at least 80 languages. The satiric adventures of the noble, demented knight and his protective squire still resonate in a world where idealism continues to tilt against corruption and materialism.

from noon to 4pm and 8 to 11pm. Closed for Sunday dinner.

Retrace your steps to the corner and turn right on Calle de San Agustín. Up ahead, the neoclassical building with substantial Corinthian columns and a pair of bronze lions is the:

10. **Cortes,** the national parliament. The building opened in 1850, and for much of its history, the politicians who assembled inside meekly concurred with the directives of whichever despot or monarch held office at the time. When a new parliament was freely elected after Franco's death in 1975, there were justifiable doubts that it would long survive. But by 1981, it appeared that democracy might actually take root. This eventuality provoked an attempted coup by right-wing members of the Guardia Civil, the feared paramilitary police force. The leader of this action, Colonel Tejero, charged into the deliberative chamber firing a submachine gun and held the deputies hostage while awaiting an expected military uprising. The coup was squelched, in large measure, by the efforts of the new king, Juan Carlos. Until then, there had been jokes about his prospective tenure, with references to "Juan Carlos the Brief." Only avid antimonarchists and die-hard Francoists mock the popular monarch now.

    Turn right at the corner of Plaza de las Cortes, which merges with Carrera de San Jeronimo. At the next corner is the:

11. **Palace Hotel,** one of the city's *grand dame* hostelries, which opened in 1912. That makes it two years younger than its smaller sibling, the Ritz, which you can soon see across the swirling traffic of the Paseo del Prado up ahead. They are both in the grandiose *beaux-arts* style that was preferred in the early 1900s. The central lounge of the Palace has a spectacular stained-glass dome, and the adjacent bar often attracts politicians from the Cortes who are making deals and journalists who are trying to catch snatches of their whispered conversations.

    Walk down the hill past the hotel entrance, staying on the south side of the street. This follows the perimeter of the:

12. **Plaza Cánovas del Castillo.** More of a traffic circle than a plaza, it has a 1782 marble statue of Neptune in the middle, holding a trident and standing atop rearing steeds. The fountain below was originally intended as a source of public water. Paseo del Prado is one of several contiguous segments of the principal north-south boulevard—often called simply "El Paseo."

At the corner, cross over to the tree-lined median that runs down the center of the Paseo and continue to the far side. Straight ahead is the northern end of Madrid's *numero uno* attraction, the:

13. **Museo del Prado,** one of Europe's most important art repositories. The undistinguished building in which the collection is housed was originally meant to be a museum of natural science, but it never served in that capacity. In the early 19th century it was requisitioned as a military headquarters for the French troops who occupied Madrid, and then it became an art museum in 1819. Whatever the deficiencies (and occasional strengths) of the Hapsburg and Bourbon monarchs of the 17th and 18th centuries, they or their advisers had exceptional tastes in art. Besides supporting the work of such Spanish artists as Velázquez, Zurbarán, Murillo, and Goya, they collected paintings by Flemish, Dutch, Italian, and French masters. The museum has important works by Titian, Rubens, Breugel, Dürer, and the iconoclastic Hieronymus Bosch, as well as lesser known paintings by Rembrandt and El Greco and a dazzling selection of early Gothic panels with frames that often outshine the panels themselves.

The museum's administrative missteps and miniscandals have kept local journalists busy in recent years; the endless renovations seem to have created as many new problems as they solved. What's more, the huge popularity of the museum has prompted many attempts at crowd control, none of which has proved entirely satisfactory, and the management has yet to find space to display a disproportionate share of the collection, which hasn't been on public view for decades.

The museum, which does not close for an afternoon siesta period, is open Tuesday through Saturday from 9am to

7pm and Sunday from 9am to 2pm. It is closed Monday and a few holidays, as are most of Madrid's museums.

Saving your visit for another time, continue down the Paseo in front of the museum. At the southern end of the building is the small Plaza de Murillo, with two fountains and a statue of the artist. Turn left and go over to the entrance to the:

14. **Jardín Botánico,** which was founded by Carlos III in 1774. Although at its loveliest in spring and summer, the garden has plants and shrubs on view throughout the year. Pick up a map inside the entrance gate to learn where specific flower beds and other plantings can be found. The garden is laid out in a formal French manner, and most of the trees and flowers are identified on small signs. Even if you have only a casual interest in horticulture, this is a pleasant place where you can escape awhile from the noisy streets of this route. The garden is open from 10am to 6pm in winter and from 10am until 9pm in summer.

As you exit the garden, turn left, then left again, continuing down the Paseo del Prado. At the southern end of the garden, the paseo widens into the:

15. **Glorieta del Emperador Carlos V,** a major intersection of seven avenues. For decades it was blighted by a highway overpass, which cast a gloomy shadow over the entire area. Now, the overpass has been demolished, and municipal authorities and private owners have spruced up the area's buildings. West of the plaza 1 block away is the **Centro de Arte Reina Sofía,** an old hospital that was converted into a museum of modern art. On the other side, over to the left, is the renovated and expanded **Estación de Atocha,** from which the new high-speed AVE trains depart several times daily for Seville. The interior concourse is a tourist attraction, with a lush grove of palm trees under a glass roof.

Make a sharp left on Calle Claudio Moyano. Over to the right is the side of the:

16. **Ministerio de Agricultura,** the flamboyant headquarters of the Ministry of Agriculture. High above the entrance are elaborate sculptures featuring winged creatures. The

administrators of the Prado proposed taking control of this building in order to acquire enough space to exhibit the works of art that are now in storage.

Walk up Calle Claudio Moyano, which is solidly lined with stalls and tables stocked with used and remaindered books. The avidity with which browsers pick through the piles of novels, histories, and textbooks is an encouraging rebuke to those who believe that Spain is a country of nonreaders. At the top of the slope is Calle de Alfonso XII, and on the other side, stretching from here well up to the north is the:

17. **Parque del Retiro,** with more than 300 acres of pathways, lakes, two exhibition halls, impressive stands of tall trees, statues, open-air cafés, fountains, athletic fields, and gardens. Cross the street at the light and continue on the dirt path leading diagonally from that corner into the park. This was yet another royal preserve—*retiro* means "retreat"—from which the public was excluded. Felipe IV had a palace here in the 17th century; all that remains now are a few outbuildings. Although some of the park was later opened to all Madrileños, the entire preserve didn't become city property until 1869.

Where the slope crests and flattens, you can see a series of playing fields over to the left. Walk along the bottom of the fields, perhaps pausing to watch players of all ages engage in the national game of *fútbol*. You will pass an artificial waterfall and cross over a small wooden bridge. Along here, the bold red squirrels of Retiro, with their furry outsized ears tend to approach even indifferent pedestrians in the hopes of securing an edible tidbit. Continue in this easterly direction until you reach a paved, north-south path—the Paseo del Ecuador. (Most of Retiro's walkways are named for Spain's former Latin American colonies.) Turn left (north); to the right is a grove of towering umbrella trees. At their base you will soon see a white-framed building of glass. Watch for a break in the bordering hedge and go down to the right, toward the building. On the right you will see a sign that identifies the species of birds in the park. Among them are magpies, black and white, that are as big as crows. If you would like to sit down or get something to drink, there's a small refreshment stand over

Triumphs and Travails in the Golden Triangle

Within a few short years, Madrid has become a center for the visual arts, almost rivaling Paris and London. Two important new art museums opened, both close to the inimitable Prado, forming the three points of what quickly became known as the "Golden Triangle."

The first addition was the Centro de Arte Reina Sofía, in a refurbished 18th-century hospital near the Atocha railroad station. Intended to showcase contemporary art, it was bequeathed the holdings of the moribund Museo Español de Arte Contemporáneo. While scholars agreed that only a few pieces in that collection could be deemed first-rate, at least there were some lesser works by Pablo Picasso, Joan Miró, and Salvador Dalí. A far greater boost to the Reina Sofía's prestige was achieved when it acquired Picasso's masterwork *Guernica* from the Prado.

In the meantime, protracted negotiations were under way to acquire the fabled private collection of the Swiss billionaire Baron Hans Heinrich Thyssen-Bornemisza. The government contracted to renovate the 19th-century Villahermosa Palace, catercorner from the Prado on the Plaza Canovas del Castillo. The job cost at least $45 million. Finally, the Baron agreed to sell his 800-piece collection of European masters and American modernists for one-fourth of its estimated worth, or $500 million. The new museum, named for him, became an instant success.

These two new museums were established at the expense of the Prado, whose problems have escalated. It lost *Guernica* and the Villahermosa Palace, which it had hoped to use as an annex. Efforts to expand by acquiring the nearby military museum were rebuffed. The roof sprang a leak and rain dripped into buckets only feet away from Velázquez's *Las Meninas*. Four directors arrived and left in as many years, often because they came into conflict with the new head of the Ministry of Culture.

The turmoil still continues, and the Spanish art world is unsure of what might happen next. Yet all three museums are setting new attendance records; it may take more than these troubles to tarnish the Golden Triangle.

to the left. Otherwise, continue up to the back of the glass building and go around to the right to reach the front. This is the:

18. **Palacio de Cristal** (Crystal Palace), a Victorian whimsy made of glass and enough cast iron to hold it together; it was created to exhibit rare plants for an 1887 colonial trade exposition. Restored prior to 1992, when Madrid was designated the "Cultural Capital of Europe," it faces a small ornamental lake. Wild and domestic ducks paddle around and under the spray of the vertical fountain. Dogs stand transfixed by their movements and those of the goldfish beneath them. Proceed from the front along the path going north, toward the building (about 100 yards away) that you can now see through the trees. This is the:

19. **Palacio de Velázquez,** another exhibition hall built for the 1887 exposition and recently restored. It is essentially neo-Mudejar, the style developed by Moorish artisans who remained in Spain after the Catholic reconquest of 1492. Stone griffins guard the front staircase and a band of ceramic tiles encircles the building at the top, just below the glass roof. This building is also used for temporary exhibits, which are normally changed on a quarterly basis. The hall is usually open Tuesday through Sunday from 11am to 6pm.

As you exit, turn right, toward the refreshment stand with outdoor tables at that end of the building. If you decide to stop for a drink or a bite to eat, be advised that the prices are high. As in the case of airport coffee shops, concessionaires in the park profit from their location. Take the path to the right of the stand, which merges with a more prominent paved walk that heads toward an intersection of even wider paths—the Plaza de Honduras.

The fountain at the center has a mermaid and merman at the base with cherubim on top. Up ahead on the right, however, is the centerpiece of the park, the:

20. **Estanque,** a large, rectangular artificial lake. If you walk along the front of the lake, the monument at the back will come into focus. It is as gaudily audacious as a monster wedding cake—one of those exercises in self-love often commissioned by inept, effete, and/or corrupt heads of state. In this case, the honoree is Alfonso XII, who was king from

1874 to 1885. His is the equestrian figure at the top of the central pedestal, whose base is surrounded by colonnades, stone lions, and bronze statuary. Some observers are offended by this grandiose pile. In this particular case, however, it was commissioned, not by the king himself, but by his grieving mother.

Walk along the promenade in front of the lake. On almost any day of the year, but especially on weekend afternoons, there will be many varied sights: young men awkwardly rowing young women in rental boats on the lake, musicians playing sambas and haunting Peruvian mountain songs, fortune-tellers reading tarot cards, organ-grinders with trained monkeys, gypsies with dog acts, and at least one person offering to write your entire name on a grain of rice.

At the end of the lake is the Plaza de Nicaragua, with another, more elegant fountain—this one with dolphins, sea creatures, and frogs all spouting water. Go left on the diagonal path down to the main entrance gate. It fronts on the circular Plaza de la Independencia, where, in the middle, stands:

21. **Puerta de Alcalá,** a neoclassical ceremonial gate with five portals (three arched, two squared) and Baroque sculptures arranged along the roofline. Completed during the 1759–1788 reign of Carlos III, it was part of his master plan to develop what was then the eastern edge of the city in order to balance the Royal Palace, Casa de Campo, and Plaza de Oriente on the west side. (As mentioned earlier, El Retiro was originally established to accommodate a palace.) For this and other projects, Carlos III has been acknowledged as the "mayor" of Madrid who did more than any other ruler to make the city a fitting capital.

If you are tired and want to end your walk here, there is a metro station across the plaza (Metro stop: Retiro); just walk over to the right and cross Calle de Alcalá. Otherwise, proceed to the left, following the circular plaza clockwise, crossing Calle de Alfonso XII, and then Calle de Alcalá before reaching:

22. **Calle de Serrano,** the premier shopping street in Madrid. Walk north on Serrano. At this end you will find mostly art

and rug galleries, but farther north are outlets of such luxury Spanish and international fashion houses as Charles Jourdan, Loewe, Versace, Vuitton, Cortefiel, Duran, Gucci, and Alfredo. (As you walk north, most of these stores are on the right-hand side of the street as well as on adjacent blocks to the east.) However, for now, stay on the left-hand side. After 3 blocks you will come to the:

23. **Museo Arquelógico Nacional,** one of Madrid's more prominent museums. Just inside the street entrance, to the left and down the stairs, is a mock cave. It was dug into the front lawn to provide space for a replica of the famous Paleolithic paintings at Altamira, in northwestern Spain. (The actual historic paintings can be viewed only on a highly restricted basis.) The museum's real treasures are inside. The collection includes significant artifacts of every important civilization that has lived on the peninsula for 3,000 years— Iberian, Roman, Visigoth, Moor. The best exhibit space is allotted to sculptures of the earliest inhabitants. In the gallery to the right of the main door is an exquisite life-sized bust of a 5th-century B.C. woman. She wears a striking headdress with large disks over her ears, a necklace of serpent skulls, and a mysterious Mona Lisa smile. Called the *Dama de Elche,* she was discovered in southeastern Spain, where the Iberians may have settled after crossing over from Africa. The artistry of the sculpture would tend to rule out any assumptions that the Iberians were merely primitive tribes. Other remarkable exhibits include the jewelry and crowns of the Visigothic kings and the mosaics and tools of the Romans.

As you continue north on Serrano, the next open space on your left is called the:

24. **Jardínes del Descubrimiento,** commemorating Spanish explorers and conquistadors of the New World. Despite the name, there is little here that could be described as garden-like, although there are some marvelously gnarled old olive trees. Much space has been given over to an ungainly 1970s monument to such historic figures as Colón (Columbus), de Soto, Pizarro, and Cortés. Turn left, walking through the Plaza de Colón with its statue of the explorer. Go down the steps to the left of the statue, arriving

at the southern end of a block-long waterfall that faces the Paseo de Recoletos.

Then turn left, crossing the narrow adjacent street and entering the staircase somewhat to the right that allows pedestrians to cross beneath the hectic Paseo. The tunnel emerges onto the median strip that runs down the west side of the Paseo. Turn left and left again, walking south. The imposing structure you can now see on the opposite side of the Paseo is the **Biblioteca Nacional** (the National Library). You will soon come to a belle-epoque whimsy on your right called:

☕ Take a Break El Pabellón del Espejo, Paseo de Recoletos 31 (tel. 308-2347). With its shaded terrace and air-conditioned glass-enclosed pavilion, this is one of the most popular cafés along this median, especially in summer, when they often have a piano player outside. Inside, there are two large glass chandeliers. The *tapas* aren't too expensive, and one can relax for an hour or two over coffee and cake. If both the terrace and pavilion are full, the mother bar-restaurant is just across the nearby access street. All are open daily.

Continue walking in the same direction (south). Soon you will come to:

25. **Café Gijon,** one of Madrid's classic cafés. It is still the site of daily *tertulias,* ritual gabfests where friends get together to discuss the issues of the day. If you would like to stop for a drink, be advised that the interior tends to be unusually thick with tobacco smoke.

Continue south down the Paseo. A long reflecting pool on the right will announce your arrival at the:

26. **Plaza de la Cibeles,** another major intersection for vehicular traffic, not pedestrians. Out in the center is Madrid's most beloved statue depicting Cibele (or Sybil), goddess of fertility, sitting in a chariot drawn by two lions; the statue is surrounded by a lovely fountain, all of which is usually illuminated at night. A pity that it can be approached only by dire threat to life and limb.

Three important buildings are located on this plaza. Over to the left is the extravagant structure with the concave facade—the 1918 **Palacio de Comunicaciónes**—the main post office. At the far right corner is the 1884 **Banco de España,** the central bank, which both sets the nation's monetary policies and stores its gold reserves. And on the near right corner, behind the iron fence and thickets of shrubs and trees is the 1747 **Palacio de Buenavista,** once owned by the Duchess of Alba but now the headquarters of the Ministry of Defense.

The Calle de Alcalá goes up a gradual incline, reaching the Puerta del Sol in four long blocks. Or, you might prefer to get the metro in front of the Ministry of Defense (Metro stop: Banco). If it is dusk, the sight of the illuminated Cibele may etch a visual image of Madrid in your mind that will endure long after your visit has ended.

GRANADA

Start: Torre de la Justicia.

Finish: Palacio de Carlos V.

Time: 2 to 3 hours.

Best Times: Arrive by 9am or from 2 to 4pm or in the late afternoon.

Worst Times: From 10am to 2pm, especially from late May to late September, when there are huge crowds.

T he Alhambra has not only color and fragrance but a sound of its own. At first, visitors might not notice the sound, for it reaches the senses almost subconsciously. It tumbles, ripples, drips, and burbles. Water. For the Moors, a desert people, the relative abundance of water in southern Spain made it an earthly paradise. They dug an elaborate system of canals and drains to carry it down from the Sierra Nevada and direct it through the Alhambra and the Generalife. As Washington Irving wrote in his *Tales of the Alhambra* (1829):

> [Water] *circulates throughout the palace, supplying its baths and fish-pools, sparkling in jets within its halls or murmuring in channels along the marble pavements. When it has paid its tribute to the royal pile, and visited its gardens and parterres, it flows down the long avenue leading to the city,*

Granada

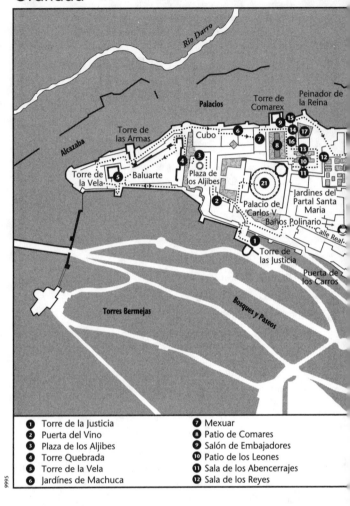

1 Torre de la Justicia	**7** Mexuar
2 Puerta del Vino	**8** Patio de Comares
3 Plaza de los Aljibes	**9** Salón de Embajadores
4 Torre Quebrada	**10** Patio de los Leones
5 Torre de la Vela	**11** Sala de los Abencerrajes
6 Jardínes de Machuca	**12** Sala de los Reyes

tinkling in rills, gushing in fountains, and maintaining a perpetual verdure in those groves that empower and beautify the whole hill of the Alhambra.

This garden of delights is now suffering from the same stresses as every other major attraction in the developed world. Tourism, simultaneously sought and deplored, brings millions of visitors to Spain each year, and more than 1½ million of them make the all-but-obligatory journey to the Alhambra. Apart from the damage produced by their mere presence, hordes of tourists all but destroy one's opportunity

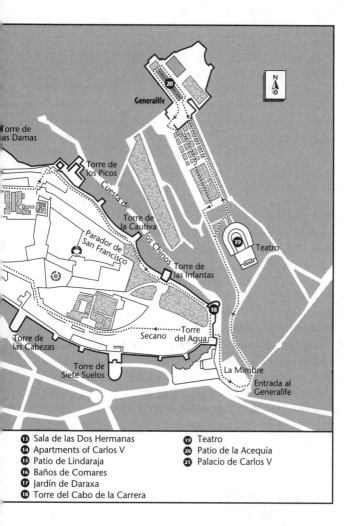

to contemplate its halls and gardens as they should be experienced—in a setting of serenity. Inevitably some rooms and areas will be closed to the public owing to renovations or simply to a need to let them rest from shuffling feet and curious fingers. The crush of tourists has also led the authorities to conduct ongoing experiments in crowd control. In both cases, micromanagement decisions lead to frequent changes, often unannounced, so the visitor using this guide needs to be flexible.

As of early 1995, the palace was open from 9am to 6pm daily plus 8 to 10pm Saturdays from October through March; from 9am to 8pm daily, plus 10pm to midnight Tuesdays, Thursdays, and Saturdays from April through September. When you get your ticket at the booth near the main gate, you will be assigned a specific 30-minute period, which is printed on your ticket. You must enter the Alcázar, or palace, during that time. Otherwise, you will have to buy another ticket for a later 30-minute period. It is best to arrive at the ticket booth before 9am so that you can enter before the morning crowds appear. Otherwise, plan to arrive during the 2 to 4pm lunch hour or in the late afternoon. Once inside, you can take as long as you like to walk through until closing time; the route connects with the gardens of the Generalife, at the eastern end of the complex.

If you enjoy hiking, you might want to walk up to the Alhambra from the city below. Whether you drive or walk, take the Cuesta de Gomérez from the Plaza Nueva, which is only 3 blocks north of Plaza Isabel la Católica, the busiest downtown intersection. The tacky souvenir shops lining the first couple of blocks dwindle as you approach the Puerta de las Granadas, a ceremonial portal built by Carlos V in the 16th century. If you are walking, enter through the gate and take the pedestrian path that veers off to the left through thick groves of trees. The steep climb to the top takes 20 to 30 minutes. If you arrive by taxi, it will continue through the gate and straight up the hill. Tell the driver to go to the:

• • • • • • • • • • • • • • • •

1. **Torre de la Justicia,** a gateway built in 1348 by Yusuf I. Above the horseshoe archway is a representation of a hand, an important Islamic symbol. The five fingers stand for the basic tenets of the faith—prayer, fasting, the giving of alms, the struggle against infidels, and the requisite pilgrimage to Mecca for all Muslims. As you enter, you will notice that the passage twists sharply to the right, then to the left, a common defensive device intended to put hostile visitors at a disadvantage. On the keystone of an inner archway you can see the engraved image of a key, employed during the wars in Spain as a countersymbol to the Christian cross. It was believed to symbolize the power of the Prophet.

As you emerge at the other end, take the brick staircase on the right, where a sign reads: *Despacho de Billetes* (ticket office). At the top, the building you see looming straight ahead is an unfinished palace that was built for Carlos V. Go around to the left, down the path to the ticket office, on the left, just beyond the palace. A sign in English explains the 30-minute rule described above and notes that visitors can request a particular half-hour during that day, subject to availablity. Otherwise, your ticket will specify the next open time slot. Carefully note your assigned time, remembering that Spaniards use the 24-hour clock.

If you have at least 30 minutes until your entry time, exit the ticket office and turn left. Straight ahead is the:

2. **Puerta del Vino** (Wine Gate). From the decorative detail, which includes a band of tiles above the arch, you can see that this portal served as a welcome—it is the gateway to the oldest part of the Alhambra.

Walk through the opening, noting a sign that reads *Alcazaba* ("fortress" in Arabic) and points to the right. The walls and towers up ahead are among the oldest structures on the hill, some of which date from the 9th century. Bear diagonally to the right, across the open space known as the:

3. **Plaza de los Aljibes** (Plaza of the Cisterns). During the Moorish reign, this was a deep ravine that served as a moat for the fort. After the Christian reconquest, large underground cisterns were installed there and then paved over. A kiosk in the middle sells drinks and a few snacks; this will be your last chance to get refreshments before entering the palace proper.

Turn left at the kiosk toward the doorway in what is known as the:

4. **Torre Quebrada** (Broken Tower). The blushing tint of the tower and its adjoining walls hints at the reason for the Arabic name for the complex—*Qal'at al-Hamra* (the "Red Citadel"). An attendant at the gate beneath the tower will punch your ticket. After visitors pass through, a sign identifies this as the *Barrio Castrense* (Military Quarter). As you turn right, you will see a staircase up ahead that goes up to a belvedere, which provides a panoramic view of the city. To continue, go to the left of the staircase and, staying to

the left, go up the winding path into a large, roughly triangular court filled with the foundations of small buildings; these were formerly the homes and workplaces of the common people who lived within the Alcazaba walls. The Alcazaba has been estimated to have had a population of 40,000 or more, primarily soldiers, their families, and supporting personnel. Stairs lead down to storage cellars and the dungeons where Christian prisoners were held. Continue across this area through the maze of low walls toward the square tower rising at the far end. Over on the left is a doorway leading to the:

5. **Torre de la Vela** (Watchtower). On the other side of that doorway and down to the left is the Jardín de los Adarves, a narrow garden along the edge of a parapet overlooking the wooded parklands below. Take a detour to the left to see the plantings beyond the bubbling fountain—rows of orange, cyprus, and palm trees above long flower beds. After taking a look, return along the path past the doorway and go up the stairs to the top of the Torre de la Vela.

This tower is the emblem of Granada, with a broad deck that permits an unobstructed sweeping view of the city. On January 2, 1492, the soldiers of the Catholic kings announced their victory over the Moors by raising their standard here, and the bell at the top has long tolled the specified hours for the irrigation of the *vega*. To the north you can see the Albaicín, an ancient *barrio* that has been significantly altered by new construction in recent decades, without regard for its history, yet achieving some measure of attractiveness. Beyond that area is Sacramonte, notorious for its numerous gypsy caves where unsuspecting tourists are all but held captive by tenacious peddlers and fortune-tellers and subjected to displays of ersatz flamenco dancing. The modern city extends in an arc from the west to the south of Albaicín, the flatlands dominated by the spires of the cathedral. Down near the Puerta de las Granadas you can see the Torres Bermejas, a small castle that once protected the old Jewish quarter.

As you descend from the watchtower, exit and bear left, past the opening where water splashes downhill, and follow the sign reading *Puerta de las Armas,* which passes through a tower of the same name. This paved path leads along the northern edge of the Alcazaba, heading back in the direction of the Plaza de los Aljibes. It ends at an elevated area at the northern end of that plaza. Continue straight across into the:

6. **Jardínes de Machuca,** which are actually a series of patios planted with olive and orange trees around a small pool. At the far side is a high wall draped with a curtain of flowering vines. Over to the right, stairs lead up into the vestibule of the first of the Arab palaces. Attendants will check your ticket to make sure you are arriving at the proper time.

Most of the Casa Real (Royal House) you are about to visit dates from the 14th century; it was ordered built between 1335 and 1410 by several princes of the ruling Nasrid dynasty. It replaced an earlier palace erected by their ancestor, Ibn el-Ahmar, who died in 1272. Open courts and inner chambers were attached to earlier buildings, with rooms clustered around central patios.

Walk ahead and turn right into a hall called the:

7. **Mexuar.** Originally, this was a council chamber, but it has been altered extensively and repeatedly. After the Christian reconquest, it was used as a chapel. At some point, a balcony called an *oratorio* was added at the far end, with a view of Albaicín. At the east end of the *oratorio* is a niche oriented toward Mecca so that the Moors could easily say their daily prayers. Recently the Mexuar has been undergoing restoration and may be closed.

Following the signs that read *Continuación Visita,* walk through the small rooms with reliefs of Arabic script and sinuous floral motifs carved in the plaster walls and enter the north end of one of the most photographed spaces in the Alhambra, the:

8. **Patio de Comares,** the famed "Court of the Myrtles." Open to the sky, the rectilinear shape of the court is accentuated by the long flat band of water that runs down the center and by the bordering hedges of sculptured myrtle. Plump crimson-and-gold carp lazily swish their fanned tails in the murk of the pool. Here, at the northern end of the court, a colonnade supporting seven arches delineates the Sala de la Barca, something of an anteroom to the:

9. **Salón de Embajadores,** beyond the loggia. This "Hall of the Ambassadors" was the site of the emir's twice-weekly audiences; although not especially large, it is one of the two most beautiful rooms in the palace. The walls sweep up 60 feet to a vaulted ceiling of carved cedar, and the walls, covered in intricate script and decorative details, meet dadoes of lustrous ceramic tiles. Portals with scalloped edges frame fragments of ramparts as well as the near and distant hills. For a hint of what such rooms may have looked like in the 14th century, imagine furnishings consisting of carpets, prayer rugs, large pillows, and low couches. Smoke probably curled from copper braziers if it was winter, and the aroma of incense and rosewater probably permeated the air. The white plaster reliefs, as well as abstract forms and shapes undoubtedly would have been gilded and painted in many bright colors, as were the marble sculptures of ancient Greece.

   As you exit the Hall of the Ambassadors, walk on the left side of the pool. Near the far end of the pool are a pair of doors that lead to the famous:

10. **Patio de los Leones** (Court of the Lions). The surrounding rooms and those on the second floor, with their wooden lattice screens, comprised the area of the king's harem. The center of the court can now be seen only through glass. In the middle are 12 stylized stone lions standing in a circle, bearing a large basin on their haunches. Jets of water arc from their mouths. In fact, they look more like large friendly hounds panting for approval than fierce beasts. For many people, the unusual nature of the sculptures is part of their appeal. But Washington Irving thought them "unworthy of their fame, being of miserable sculpture, the work probably of some Christian captive." A loggia of 124 slender marble pillars runs all around the courtyard, surmounted by intricately carved capitals and exquisite fretwork. Much of the plasterwork retains hints of the many colors that had once coated it. Protruding into the court at opposite ends are two pavilions with pyramidal cupolas above small pools. It is conjectured that these pillars and carvings were meant to represent the palm trunks and foliage of ancestral desert oases.

Walk around the court in a counterclockwise direction. There are important chambers off each side of the court. The first, on the south side, is the:

11. **Sala de los Abencerrajes.** It is alleged that a number of executions and assorted homicides took place here, including the assassination of an entire family of presumed conspirators. The room is named for them. Some exuberant guides claim that the red stains seen running from the low fountain at the center of the room originated from the blood of the victims, but actually these are residues of iron oxide.

    As you exit this room, continue to the right. At the east end of the courtyard, past the pavilion, is the:

12. **Sala de los Reyes** (Hall of the Kings). Notice the ceiling paintings on leather that depict life at the court of the emirs. Since Islamic law doesn't permit artistic renditions of human beings, it is assumed that these were rendered by a Christian artist at the end of the Moorish rule or perhaps following the Christian reconquest.

    Exit this room and continue to the right, entering the:

13. **Sala de las Dos Hermanas** (Hall of the Two Sisters), named for the pair of marble slabs set into the floor, or, possibly, for two of the sultan's favorite wives. A window at the back faces an enclosed garden. Overhead is a domed ceiling honeycombed with thousands of cells formed by delicate protuberances dripping down like dainty stalactites. Nowhere in the palace is it more obvious that the emirs built it simply for their own pleasure. The decorative material is made of highly fragile sculptured plaster. It is astonishing that the material has survived centuries of neglect and abuse after the reconquest until serious renovation efforts were begun in the mid-19th century. Much has been lost, but this room and a few others hint at the former splendor.

    Exit through the small doorway with the pointed arch, where you will see another *Continuación Visita* sign. You will be in a corridor with beams above and shuttered windows on the right, which will take you to a room with a deeply coffered ceiling that is clearly not Moorish. This room is part of the:

Perfumed Nights

Washington Irving was only one of several notables who celebrated the wonders of the Alhambra. By the time he arrived, the palace had endured centuries of neglect and abuse. Earthquakes and explosions had taken their toll. Carlos V tore down parts of the palace in order to build one of his own, and Napoleon's troops looted it and even tried to blow it up in the early 19th century. Vagabonds lived in its splendid rooms, lighting fires to cook their food. Smugglers pursued their trade there, and thieves set up their market for stolen goods.

Still, traveling artists, poets, and writers loosely associated with the Romantic movement of the first half of the 19th century saw the beauty beneath the grime and decay. Their writings prompted the Spanish government to initiate restoration efforts that continue to this day. Other celebrated visitors included Theóphile Gautier, a French writer, and Benjamin Disraeli, the future prime minister of Great Britain. Disraeli, who saw the Alhambra a year after Irving, exclaimed that the site was "the most delicate and fantastic creation that ever sprang up in a fairy tale."

Even more smitten was the novelist Alexandre Dumas, who stopped here in 1846 during a grand tour. Upon his arrival in Granada, he saw a city that was like "a sleepy maiden resting in the sunshine on a bed of moss and bracken, ringed round with cactus plants and aloes." Of the Generalife, he proclaimed that "nowhere in the world will you find in such a small expanse such fragrance, such freshness, such a multitude of windows, each opening on a corner of paradise." At that time Dumas was at the height of his considerable popularity, and his praise carried great weight. Spain, especially the region of Andalucia (which includes Granada), soon experienced what could be described as its first tourist boom of the modern era.

14. **Apartments of Carlos V,** which were adapted to his taste in the early 16th century, about 35 years after his grandparents staged their victory march into Granada. Three

centuries later, these rooms were lent to Washington Irving during his brief tenure as an American consular official in Granada in 1829. Here he wrote *Tales of the Alhambra.* During his stay, the household chores were in the capable hands of "the chatelaine Doña Antonia," her niece "the plump little black-eyed Dolores," and a "tall, stuttering, yellow-haired lad named Pépe" who worked in the gardens of the palace. A marble plaque on the wall of a second large room attests to Irving's stay here. He is given substantial credit for motivating the Spanish government to preserve what was left of the Nasrid residences.

After you exit along an elevated walkway open on both sides, go down to an enclosed garden, the:

15. **Patio de Lindaraja,** with orange and stately cypress trees. Bear right along the edge of the patio, and up ahead are the:

16. **Baños de Comares** (Royal Baths). In recent years, they have been closed to the public from January to April, as part of a preservation effort. When open, they reveal cool vaulted chambers that remind one of the sensual orientalism depicted by the European Romantic painters of the first half of the 19th century. Some of these painters were actually inspired by the Alhambra. If the baths are closed, a fenced opening to the right will provide a hint of what lies beyond.

Proceed ahead out into the:

17. **Jardín de Daraxa,** the first of many terraced gardens that lie to the east of the palace. Up ahead you can see a long rectangular reflecting pool, guarded at the south end by two stone lions that spout water. These are more recent than those in the Court of the Lions. At the other end of the pool is an open pavilion, the Tower of the Women, which provides yet another vista of Albaicín.

As you continue in the same easterly direction, following the *Continuacíon Visita* signs, stroll through the Partal Gardens, staying to the left of the northern perimeter wall, with its several watchtowers. Throughout these stepped gardens, it will be obvious that the Moors delighted in the profligate use of water, with many pools, troughs, rivulets, and gentle cascades blending their gurgles with birdsong.

Soon, the path passes beneath the terrace of the Parador de San Francisco on the right, which is inaccessible from this side. This was a Christian monastery ordered built by Isabel and Fernando after the reconquest. She was buried for a while in one of the monastery's patios until her remains were removed to the royal chapel adjoining the cathedral down in the city. After the Torre de la Cautiva and the Torre de las Infantas, the path enters the shade of a double row of cypresses. The next fortification on the wall is the:

18. **Torre del Cabo de la Carrera,** literally, the "Tower of the End of the Track." It marks the end of the palace grounds but not the end of the attraction. A little farther on is a gate on the left that allows access to a viaduct that spans a deep ravine. Cross the viaduct and follow the path up to the left; it leads toward the grounds of the summer residence of the Moorish kings, the Generalife (pronounced "Hay-nay-ral-EE-fay"). Far from having a militaristic connotation, Generalife means "Gardens of Paradise."

Soon, on the right, you will come to an open-air:

19. **Teatro.** Concerts are held here in the summer; it is one of several venues in the Alhambra for the annual Music and Dance Festival, held from mid-June through early July. The famed "Three Tenors"—José Carreras, Luciano Pavarotti, and Placido Domingo—have all appeared here.

Go to the right, around the back of the theater, and walk up the stairs between the pair of vertical fountains into a section of high hedges clipped in the shape of fortified walls. Two long reflecting pools mark the center of this court. By stairs and slopes, the paths later converge on a pavilion that anchors the southern end of the:

20. **Patio de la Acequia.** This long open court is flanked by arcades draped in bougainvillea and other flowering vines. Down the sides are luxuriant gardens of roses, geraniums, salvias, and oleander, punctuated by orange and myrtle trees. But what draws and holds visitors' attention is the narrow pool that runs more than 160 feet down the center of the space, for scores of high thin jets of water form a canopy above the length of the pool, tapering at the apex of their

arc and falling back into the pool. You can hear the sound long before you can see the fountains, a fittingly musical denouement to this stroll among the playing grounds of the Moors. You can linger here as long as you like. When you are ready to leave, retrace your steps back down through the gardens, perhaps taking the high path to the left for a different perspective. All paths lead down to the bridge back across to the Alhambra grounds. This time, though, go to the left, past the cannon. This path is partially bordered by cypress hedges. Over to the left are the much-restored outer walls; to the right, the gardens of the *parador.* Near the end of the path, where you will see ruined building foundations to the left, is a sign that reads: *Palacio de los Abencerrajes.* These are ongoing excavations of another (presumably earlier) palace: what has been uncovered so far include low walls, tile floors, and a few staircases leading nowhere.

Leave the grounds by way of the iron gate, which you will see just ahead.

Take a Break There are no opportunities to buy food or beverages inside the palace or the Generalife, but several options are available outside the iron gate. Over to the right is the entrance to the:

Parador de San Francisco, Calle Real s/n (tel. 221-440). Dating from the early 15th century, this former monastery is one of the two most popular inns of a national chain (the other is in Toledo). Attractively furnished in period style, it preserves several patios and a large interior court. One of these spaces was the temporary resting place of Isabel. Although room reservations must be made months in advance, the public is welcome to dine in the restaurant, or order a drink and a sandwich at the bar or out on the large terrace, with its inviting views of the hills and gardens.

Or walk down to the left from the iron gate, away from the parador. Over to the right is the modest:

Hostal América, Calle Real (tel. 227-471). Past the amusingly furnished front parlor is a court where hearty, home-style three-course meals are available from March through November. It is closed December through February.

If you continue down the same street, on the left you will find the:

Polinario Cafetéria, Calle Real. Sandwiches, *tapas,* and drinks are available at the bar in front; the patio restaurant in back serves an inexpensive buffet lunch. It's open during the same hours as the palace.

One prominent building remains to be visited. Down on the right, near the ticket office, is the:

21. **Palacio de Carlos V.** Its thick, rusticated stone walls exemplify the Spanish Renaissance style, which is ponderous and imposing, and in sharp contrast to the delicacy of the almost whimsical residences of the emirs. At least some of the Moorish buildings that still existed 34 years after the Christian victory had to be razed in order to accommodate this palace, which was never completed. This will be evident as soon as you enter through the doorway around to the right. The circular opening in the roof was meant to be covered with a dome, but this was never built. The explanation given for not completing the palace is that it was threatened by earthquakes while under construction. At various times, the building has been used as a bullring, for musical performances, and for other celebrations. The side galleries house two small museums; the most interesting one is the Museo Hispano-Musulman, which displays relics discovered in the Alhambra over the centuries. Included are pottery collections, distinctive marquetry furniture and accessories, and architectural and sculptural fragments. The undisputed treasure is an amphora of blue glass more than 4 feet high that once stood in the Hall of the Two Sisters. The second museum specializes in religious paintings of the Christian era. Both museums are open from 10am to 2pm Tuesday through Sunday.

As you exit the palace, the staircase down to the Torre de la Justicia is over to the left.

CÓRDOBA

Start: Outside La Mezquita.

Finish: Puente Romano.

Time: 2 to 3 hours, not including rest stops.

Best Times: Daily 10:30am to 1:30pm and 4 to 7pm from May through September; 10:30am to 1:30pm and 3:30 to 5:30pm October through March.

Worst Times: Any time other than the hours listed above, which are when Córdoba's main attraction, La Mezquita, is open.

Andalucía used to be an independent country. What is now an eight-province region stretching almost 350 miles across southern Spain was known to the Moors as "al-Andalus." While they once ruled all of Iberia, and even crossed the Pyrenees into France, they remained here the longest. From the mid-8th century until the end of the 13th, Córdoba was their capital.

Succeeding dynasties—the Ommayyads, the fundamentalist Almoravides, and the fanatical Almohades—proclaimed their suzerainty by constructing more than 250,000 mosques, palaces, bathhouses, shops, and homes. Little of that legacy remains, owing to revolts and acts of vengeance as well as the disdain and neglect of the Christians who reclaimed the land. What does remain, therefore, is all the more valuable.

Córdoba

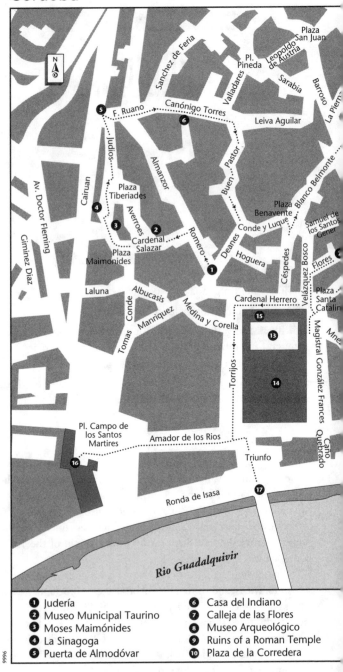

1. Judería
2. Museo Municipal Taurino
3. Moses Maimónides
4. La Sinagoga
5. Puerta de Almodóvar
6. Casa del Indiano
7. Calleja de las Flores
8. Museo Arqueológico
9. Ruins of a Roman Temple
10. Plaza de la Corredera

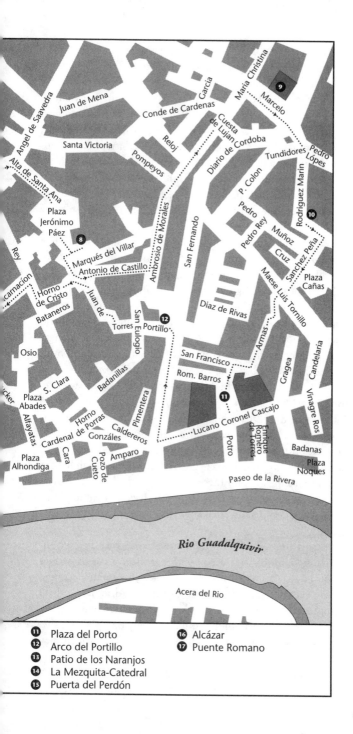

A mere hint of the grandeur that was the Córdoba of the Moors can be visited on the western outskirts of the present city. Medina Azahara was a storied summer resort begun in 936 by a caliph who named the complex for a favorite wife. It is claimed that his palace atop the hill had 400 rooms, and it was surrounded by a virtual city of schools, shops, stables, barracks, fountains, ponds, minarets, and a mosque, all lavishly constructed and appointed with materials imported from hundreds of miles away. These buildings accommodated 12,000 soldiers, 4,000 servants, the royal family and the members of their court, and necessary support personnel—a total of about 25,000 people. That, by itself, is remarkable enough. But if the accounts that have been passed down are true, all these people were housed under one roof, supported by more than 4,300 columns!

Now, only one's active imagination can conjure up such magnificence. Although sporadic renovations and reconstructions try to depict the outlines of the site, the only tangible remains are foundations and truncated sections of the roof and floors. About the only way to visualize what Medina Azahara must have looked like is to visit the one remaining major Moorish structure in Córdoba—the Great Mosque or *Mezquita.*

Even that fabulous building, which covers 6 acres, requires some effort on the part of those who would like to understand Moorish culture. It was allowed to fall into disrepair after the Christian reconquest; nearly all its 28 entrances were crudely blocked off and a grotesquely out-of-place cathedral punched into an unfeeling gash in its heart. Yet the Mezquita still has the power to inspire awe, for there is nothing quite like it anywhere else in the Western world. Even that misbegotten church in its midst has a compelling resonance, if only to provide a ghastly contrast.

Apart from the Mezquita, there are relatively few monuments in Córdoba. It is a city with a densely textured history but not much to show for it. Its few museums are modest, and the only other significant structure is the Alcázar, a hybrid 13th-century Christian castle that incorporates remnants of Roman and Moorish buildings that formerly occupied the site. It has been undergoing renovation in recent years, which may not yet be finished.

Although Córdoba does have other attractions, weary sightseers might enjoy spending additional leisure time relaxing at sidewalk cafés and browsing in fetching shops tucked into corners of pocket plazas. Córdobese artisans still produce delicately wrought silverware and the embossed, gilded leatherwork called *guadamecil*. To see their work, simply explore the labyrinthine lanes of the Judería, the old Jewish quarter of whitewashed houses that surrounds the major Muslim attraction.

The following itinerary will save the key attraction—the Mezquita— for last but enable you to reach it at least an hour before closing time.

● ● ● ● ● ● ● ● ● ● ● ● ● ● ● ●

Start at the intersection of Calle Torrijos and Calle Cardenal Herrero, at the northwest corner of the Mezquita. Walk to the west, along a short block of gaudy souvenir shops, turning right on Calle Deanes and then, a few steps later, left at the "Y" intersection onto Calle Almanzor Romero. This is the:

1. **Judería** (Jewish quarter). Most of the modest buildings here date from the 18th century or later, but they resemble the older Córdoba. A few scattered buildings predate 1492 when Isabel and Fernando proclaimed the edict that led to the Sephardic diaspora of the 16th century.

At the next corner, turn left into the Plaza Cardenal Salazar. Passing a battered former chapel on your right, continue into the connecting Plazuela de Maimónides. On the right is the:

2. **Museo Municipal Taurino,** a museum of bullfighting housed in a pair of attractive adjoining mansions. Inside are mementoes of such bullfighting luminaries as Manolete and the colorful native son El Cordobés. The museum is open Tuesday through Sunday, and its hours vary somewhat according to the season.

Go around the museum to the right, into the Plaza Tiberiades, where you will see a statue of:

3. **Moses Maimónides,** a Jew in a Muslim city who achieved high honor as a physician, theologian, and philosopher. He is shown sitting on a bench, a book in his lap and a turban on his head, as if in contemplation before meeting with a patient or a student. Córdoba was not a uniformly tolerant

city, although Muslims, Christians, and Jews did live in relative peace throughout much of its history. Because Maimónides experienced persecution during the 12th century, he traveled around the Mediterranean area in search of work and acceptance. He found both in Egypt, where he died in 1204. His writings demonstrated an astonishing breadth of knowledge, including medicine, philosophy, public health, law, logic, and religion.

Not far beyond the statue, on the left along Calle Judios, you will see the entrance to:

4. **La Sinagoga,** one of only three intact synagogues remaining in Spain. (The other two are in Toledo; however, fragments of what may have been synagogues have been unearthed in other towns and cities, including Girona, north of Barcelona.) This one dates from the 14th century and has decidedly Middle Eastern embellishments in its intricately carved plasterwork; on the walls are quotations from the Psalms written in Hebrew. The building consists of a small, square room, above which is the *ezrat nashim,* the traditional segregated balcony for women and girls. Although no longer used for worship, the synagogue is open Tuesday through Saturday from 10am to 2pm and 3:30 to 5:30pm. It is closed Sunday afternoon and Monday and has extended afternoon hours during the summer.

Continue in the same direction along Judios. At the end, turn left, through the:

5. **Puerta de Almodóvar,** a Moorish gate at the western edge of the Judería. On the other side, next to a park that borders a section of Moorish fortifications, is a statue of Lucius Annaeus Seneca. Born in Córdoba in 4 B.C., a citizen of Rome, he was such an esteemed intellectual that Nero appointed him as his personal counselor. When the emperor became disenchanted with Seneca's advice, he ordered the philosopher to kill himself, which he did, in A.D. 65.

Roman paganism and Judaism are represented by the statues of Maimónides and Seneca. To see a likeness of the third pillar of Córdoba's intellectual triumvirate, you can make a detour down to the left along the wall. After about 2 blocks you will see a statue of Maimónides's Muslim contemporary and mirror-image, Averroës. A physician, philosopher, and writer, he, too, was persecuted at the hands of reactionary Moorish authorities; he went into exile in Morocco as an aide to a sultan.

Whether or not you make this detour, walk back through the Puerta de Almodóvar into the Judería, along Calle F. Ruano. This street soon opens into a plaza with orange trees. On the right is an architectural oddity, the:

6. **Casa del Indiano.** The ground floor exterior is Mudejar, a Moorish style produced by Arabs who came under Christian rule, while the carvings around the two windows on the upper floor are Isabeline—a florid decorative mode named for Queen Isabel—that was popular for a couple of decades after the Moors were defeated in 1492.

Continue in the same direction; the street is now called Canonigo Torres. Turn right on Buen Pastor, which slopes slightly downhill, then turn left on Calle Conde y Luque. This soon opens into the Plaza Benavente. Turn slightly to the right, cross the plaza, and enter the narrow passageway on the opposite side. A few steps later, turn right into Calle Velázquez Bosco. Half a block farther, on the left, will bring you to an even narrower lane, the:

7. **Calleja de las Flores.** Enter this lane, where you will pass a workshop—the Taller Meryan—whose artisans create embossed leather goods, a craft for which Córdoba has long been recognized. At the end is a compact plaza with a small fountain. The alley is appropriately named, for it is decked with cascades of blossoming vines and pots of flowers much of the year. Once you are in the plaza, turn around and look at the steeple of the cathedral framed between the stuccoed houses. Photographs from this perspective appear on every postcard stand in town.

If you choose, you could cut this walk short by turning left from the alley on Velázquez Bosco. This will bring you to Cardenal Herrero and the northeast corner of the Mezquita. About 20 yards straight ahead is the entrance to the Mosque. If you prefer to enter it now, skip ahead to Stop no. 14.

Otherwise, go to Velázquez Bosco and turn right, retracing your steps to the Plaza Benavente. Turn right and go up the hill on Blanco Belmonte. The street names are

Fiesta of the Patios

After the Great Mosque, visitors are most likely to remember Córdoba for its patios. Although they may appear to be quintessentially Spanish, they are actually Moorish in origin. The Moors were not accomplished architects (at least when compared with their predecessors in Spain, the Romans), but they understood how to deal with dry climates and the sun's heat. This is evident in the simple but effective floor plans of even the humblest houses, a layout that is still used, especially in the Judería.

The central feature of each house is the inner court—the patio. It is surrounded by high walls, which help to retain the coolness of the night. Overhead awnings controlled by ropes and pulleys deflect the direct rays of the sun, and the near-universal fountains and garden pools provide mental refreshment. Flowers in jugs, trees in vats, and greenery climbing up walls also produce a restorative effect, even on sweltering days.

In Córdoba the patio is the living room of the home (or homes, as when neighbors in adjacent houses jointly maintain a single courtyard). And this living room is open to a broad range of friends. Variations on the common Spanish sentiment *mi casa es su casa* ("my house is your house") are frequently spoken here, as when strangers peek in doorways and look as if they would like to enter.

This is a common occurrence in early May, a month of many celebrations in Córdoba, especially the Festival de los Patios. Residents make a special effort to fill every patio with lush, eye-filling floral displays, hang their walls with rows of flower-filled pots, and cover their floor tiles with blankets of colorful vegetation. The results are there for all to admire, for even the patios that are normally closed to curious passersby are opened. Visitors who are invited to enter can walk about and exclaim. It is polite to smile often at the hosts and to shower them with compliments. Be sure to keep an eye out for the discreet little plate or basket with money in it. Contributing a 50-peseta coin or two will help the hosts defray the cost of their display.

often changed in this area, and official efforts to keep the street signs up to date leave much to be desired. Near the top of this hill a wide spot is identified as Angel de Saavedra, with an undistinguished church on the right. Turn right and go down the alley that borders the north side of the church, walking along Alta de Santa Ana.

This short stretch is relatively peaceful and quiet. Follow it and go down several long flights of stairs into the Plaza Jerónimo Páez. You will see benches arranged in the shade of orange, pine, and palm trees. Walk through the plaza, where groups of students and neighborhood residents often relax. Over to the left is the entrance to the:

8. **Museo Arqueológico,** which is housed in an impressive Renaissance mansion. Among its carefully mounted exhibits are artifacts from the prehistoric to Gothic periods in Córdoba province, including Roman mosaics, Visigothic artworks, and Moorish relics. The museum is open Tuesday through Saturday from 10am to 2pm and from 5 to 7pm; on Sundays and holidays from 10am to 1:30pm.

Cross the plaza and turn left on Calle Antonio de Castillo (not the sharper left on Marqués de Villar). This will bring you to Plaza Seneca. Turn left along Calle Ambrosio de Morales, which eventually intersects with the heavily congested Calle Claudio Marcelo. Look down to the right. At the next corner, on the opposite side, you can see the:

9. **Ruins of a Roman Temple,** made up primarily of 11 fluted columns. Turn right and walk down Claudio Marcelo, cross over the five-street intersection (carefully!), and bear right down Calle Rodrigues Marin. Very shortly, on the right, you will come to a block called Tundidores. Up on the left is:

Take a Break Taberna Salinas, Tundidores 3 (tel. 480-135). In business since 1879, this atmospheric tavern has a bar with bullfighting memorabilia and wine casks installed in the wall behind the counter. A list of *raciones* suggests gazpacho, croquettes, and marinated anchovies as possible snacks. Full meals in the adjoining dining room are traditional and relatively inexpensive. Open Monday through Saturday from noon to 4pm and 7 to midnight.

Return to Rodrigues Marin and turn right, proceeding downhill. This street turns left at the bottom and goes through a gate into the:

10. **Plaza de la Corredera,** an arcaded square that dates from the late 17th century. It is the only enclosed plaza in Andalucía, an appropriate venue for the autos-da-fé, bullfights, and other *manifestaciónes populares.* Today there is an open food market most week day mornings. Despite periodic restoration efforts, the square remains somewhat disheveled.

Leave the plaza through the portal on the south side. Take the street directly ahead called Sanchez Peña, which crosses the small Plaza de las Cañas followed by Calle Maese Luis and then becomes Calle Armas. Walk right a few steps on Calle San Francisco, then left at the next corner into the graceful:

11. **Plaza del Porto** (Colt Square), which can easily be identified by the fountain in the center with a statue of a horse. On the left-hand side is the **Museo de Bellas Artes,** in a former late 15th-century hospice that may have been one of the places where Queen Isabel and King Fernando granted audiences to Columbus. It now houses less important works by Goya, Murillo, and Zurbarán, among others. It is open from 10am to 2pm and 6 to 8pm (5 to 7pm in the winter); it is closed Sunday afternoons and Mondays in the summer. The galleries in the northern section of the building house works by the inexplicably popular 20th-century Córdoban artist, Julio Romero de Torres, who specialized in portraits of dark-eyed *señoritas* of sultry demeanor and uncertain virtue.

On the opposite side of the plaza is a former *posada* where Cervantes once stayed. He mentioned the inn and this plaza in *Don Quijote,* a fact proudly proclaimed on a nearby plaque. The *posada* now displays items of embossed leatherwork.

Walk to the end of the square and turn right on Calle Lucano. After 1 block, turn right on Calle San Fernando (a street lined with orange trees). After 2 blocks, on the left, you will come to the:

12. **Arco del Portillo,** formerly a gate in the ancient city walls. Go through the gate. At the end of that short street, in front of the Hostal El Portillo, cut to the right a few steps, then left on to Calle Juan de Torres, following the sign that reads *A la Mezquita y Barrio Judería.* Although this street ends at the Plaza Jerónimo Páez, turn left before reaching it—on to Calle Horno de Cristo. At the end of this street turn right, then quickly left again on to Calle de la Encarnación. This will lead you back to the street where this walk began—Cardenal Herrero. Straight ahead is the northeast corner of the Great Mosque. Turn left along that wall and go down Calle Magistral González Francés to the entrance known as St. Catherine's Gate, in the wall to your right. Step inside to the:

13. **Patio de los Naranjos** (Court of the Orange Trees). Before approaching the ticket booth and entrance to the Mezquita (over to the left), stroll around this courtyard. You will notice low walls beneath rows of orange trees where one can stop to rest. Close to the far opposite corner you can see the Christian belfry tower that was mounted atop the old minaret. During Muslim times, the fountains situated around the court were used for ritual bathing. None of this, however, will prepare you for the Mezquita itself—perhaps the most significant single structure of Moorish Spain.

When you are ready, buy your ticket and enter at the doorway near St. Catherine's Gate. The complete and official name of this building is:

14. **La Mezquita-Catedral.** Although most of the structure is Moorish in origin, it has served as a Catholic cathedral since the 16th century. In a curious way, that decision by the bishops of Carlos V actually saved this monument of singular artistry.

It will take a few minutes for your eyes to adapt to the darkness inside. The absence of light is one of the consequences that resulted when this mosque was turned into a place of Christian worship. During the centuries of Moorish rule, there were at least 28 portals along the four sides of the rectangular building. This gave parishoners ready access to the mosque from all directions five times a day. Now, all except two of the entrances have been sealed off with bricks; that explains the patched, closed-off appearance of the exterior. As your eyes become accustomed to the dark, you will be able to comprehend the humbling vastness of the space and the unique way it has been formed.

A flat roof covers nearly 6 acres of floor space. It is supported by what is routinely (and aptly) described as a "forest" of some 850 pillars stretching off into the murk at the distant corners. Those columns (the exact number is not known) support double arches, some of which have scalloped edges and all with alternating bands of white stone and brick. The pillars are made from a variety of materials, including marble, granite, onyx, limestone, and even wood. Since no two are exactly alike in shape, diameter, or height, there is no chance of numbing uniformity.

Turn left from the entrance and walk toward the south wall. About halfway across, turn right, toward the center. The stunning magnitude of the building will now become even more obvious. And soon you will see something else—an almost unimaginable intrusion, a desecration in the opinion of many. It is a **Cathedral,** a grotesque tribute to Gothic-Rococo excess plunked down in the middle of a monument characterized by structural lightness and sparse decoration.

Bishops of the Church Triumphant obtained the permission of Carlos V to convert this Muslim house of worship into a cathedral. If this edifice exemplified *good* Baroque style, one might excuse it, but this agglomeration of marble saints, coffered ceilings, rampant cherubim, and curls of stucco, alabaster, and jasper would stand as a visual insult almost anywhere. When Carlos V came to see the structure that he had authorized, he said in effect: "What you have made here may be found in many places, but what you have destroyed is to be found nowhere else in the world."

Many have concurred with that sentiment, even though uttered by a king who had ordered significant destruction of Moorish monuments (including a wide swath through the Alhambra in Granada). Once one has conceded the ugliness of the cathedral, it must be acknowledged that such destruction had been carried out by others as well.

When the Moors conquered most of Spain in the early 8th century, those who settled in Córdoba shared a Visigothic church with its Christian congregation. By 785, additional space was needed. The presiding caliph ordered the church razed, except for the interior pillars, most of which had been salvaged from Roman temples and earlier Visigothic churches. During three subsequent expansions, these columns were supplemented by others scavenged from pagan and Christian sites all over Spain and North Africa, as well as France and Turkey. In that sense, superimposing the cathedral upon the mosque was simply part of the natural order of conquest and migration; each newly dominant culture built upon, and borrowed from, its predecessors. Perhaps one might conclude that the Christians had actually showed admirable restraint in sparing the Mezquita from all except a few modifications from the time they retook Córdoba in 1236 until the cathedral was begun about 1520.

After you pass the midpoint of the cathedral, look slightly to the left where you will see a **Capilla Real** (Royal Chapel). Completed in the 14th century, it was decorated in the Mudejar manner. Actually its hybrid style is not entirely incompatible with either the cathedral or the mosque.

From the chapel, turn left. The second caliph who ordered an addition to the Mosque also commissioned its most dazzling component. It can be seen in the south wall, glowing in the shadows—the holiest place in any mosque, the **Mihrab.** Golden, glittery mosaic tiles encase the triple-domed enclosure known as the *maksourah,* which is reserved for the caliph. The mihrab itself is a niche off this vestibule, its entrance formed by marble columns that support entwined arches. The whole gleams like a bejeweled necklace lying on black velvet. Its beauty is enough to make even the faithful excuse the fact that, owing the builders' to miscalculation, the mihrab is oriented toward the south, rather than to the east and Mecca.

Turn around and walk north, past the western end of the cathedral proper. This is the original mosque, which was begun in 785. Variations in the columns are more evident here. Near the north wall, turn right (east) and return to the main entrance. As you exit, turn left and walk across the courtyard to the:

15. **Puerta del Perdón** (Gate of Pardon or Forgiveness), whose entrance is in the north wall at the base of the minaret/belfry. You might like to climb to the top for a view of the city and river. As you exit, you will go through the bronze doors into Calle Cardenal Herrero. Turn left and a few steps farther on the right is an alley leading to the entrance of:

> **Take a Break** El Caballo Rojo, Cardenal Herrero 28 (tel. 475-375). Many believe that The Red Horse is the city's top restaurant. Its management takes pride in its re-creation of ancient Moorish and Jewish recipes. The bar at the end of the entryway stays open somewhat longer than the dining rooms—from about 1 to 5pm and 8pm to midnight. Drinks, sandwiches, and *tapas* are available, and the air-conditioning is a relief on a summer day.

You may prefer to end your walk here. But, if you would like to continue, exit El Caballo Rojo, turn right and then go left down Calle Torrijos. At the end, turn right on Calle Amador de los Rios. After 1 block, on the left, you will reach the:

16. **Alcázar,** a fortified royal residence whose walls and floors (from the Roman era) and patios (from a Moorish fortress) were incorporated into this structure for the Catholic monarch, Alfonso XI. The palace has terraced gardens that make use of running water in many soothing ways. Since the palace has been undergoing renovation, however, it may not be open to the public.

Return to Torrijos, turn right (past the monument to San Rafael), go down Calle Triunfo past the Puerta del Puente (Bridge Gate), and cross the busy Ronda de Isasa to the:

17. **Puente Romano.** If you walk out onto the Roman Bridge about 50 yards, you will have a photogenic view of the south side of the Mezquita and the old town, and, over to your left, the reconstructed Moorish water wheel.

SEVILLE

Start: Plaza de San Francisco.

Finish: Plaza de España.

Time: 3 hours, not including rest stops.

Best Times: Any day from 9am to 1pm and 4 to 7pm April through October, 9am to 2pm November through March.

Worst Times: Siesta periods (from 1:30 to 4pm) and Sundays, when most shops and other sites are closed; winter evenings after 5pm.

The enigma that is Spain is perhaps most evident in the quintessentially Spanish Seville. Whether the city is approached from the air or by road, the surrounding countryside often looks bleak and arid, and yet there are olive and orange groves as well as vegetable farms. With nearly 60 churches and one of the largest cathedrals in the world, Seville's population is profoundly religious. This is also evident in the pre-Easter period, when penitents drag heavy chains and crosses through the streets for hours while flagellants exorcise their demons. Afterward, however, there is a week of joyous festivities (some might call them debaucheries) that seem to encourage people to sin again so that they can be forgiven once more the following year. In 1936, when the Falangist revolt flared in Seville,

Seville

1. Plaza de San Francisco
2. Patio de los Naranjos
3. Plaza de la Virgen de los Reyes
4. Giralda
5. Catedral
6. Barrio Santa Cruz
7. Plaza Santa Cruz
8. Jardínes de Murillo
9. Plaza de los Venerables
10. Plaza Doña Elvira
11. Plaza de Alianza
12. Plaza del Triunfo
13. Alcázar
14. Museo de Arte Contemporaneo
15. Casa Lonja
16. Torre del Oro
17. Teatro de la Maestranza
18. Plaza de Toros de la Maestranza
19. Puente de Isabel II
20. Hotel Alfonso XIII
21. University
22. Plaza de España

leftist workers at first armed themselves to resist and then decided to burn 11 churches to the ground while the Rebels took control of the city—a somewhat curious tactical decision. At times Sevillanos can seem impossibly provincial, as if they were reluctant to abandon the 19th century. Then they embraced progress with their concerted effort to assure the success of Expo '92—a paean to the future.

You can detect these contrasts, if not completely understand them, by walking among the people of this sometimes

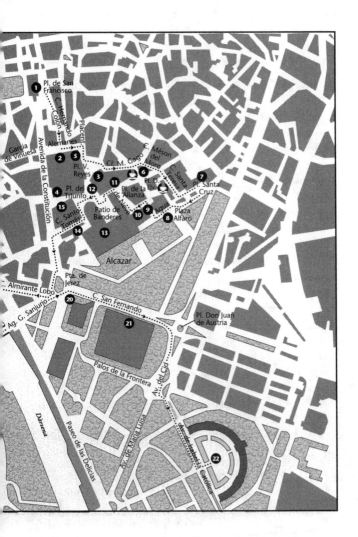

baffling but always endearing city. Seville is divided by a long looping curve in the Guadalquivir River, which is kept navigable by frequent dredging. Most of the principal attractions, including the Giralda, Alcázar, Catedral, and the Barrio Santa Cruz, are clustered on the east side of the river. The more modern districts are on the western side but, except for a strip along the central section of the river, are of little interest to the average visitor.

• • • • • • • • • • • • • •

Our walking tour begins near the center of monumental Seville, in the:

1. **Plaza de San Francisco,** behind the **Ayuntamiento** (City Hall). This square is essentially reserved for pedestrians, with vehicles routed around one side. Face the back of the Ayuntamiento. This east side is as florid and overwrought with decoration as the west side is austere. The Plateresque style in vogue when the building was constructed (1534) was so named because its carvings of cherubs, portraits, and medallions entwined with vine and floral motifs resembled the intricate silverwork (*plata,* "silver") of the period. Restoration began too late to save much of the facade (look at the blank wall at the north end), but at least what has survived will give you an idea of what the original probably looked like.

Still facing the city hall, look right (north). Up at that end of the elongated plaza is the beginning of Calle de las Sierpes (Street of the Serpents) a popular shopping street that also accommodates Seville's many processions, especially during Holy Week. Now look to the left; you will see a steeple with a weathervane thrusting skyward that dominates the surrounding buildings. That's the Giralda, which is visible throughout the city. Walk in that direction—down Calle Hernando Colón, with its mix of quirky shops and cafés. After 1 block, on the opposite side of Calle Alemanes, you will see the entrance to the:

2. **Patio de los Naranjos** (Patio of the Orange Trees). Repairs and renovations often keep the patio closed to visitors. But, according to an unpredictable schedule that fluxuates at the whim of functionaries, this gate is sometimes open, so that you can enter a vestibule from which you can view the patio. Out in the middle, surrounded by the trees, is the fountain where the Moors performed their obligatory ablutions. At the far side is the northern wall of the cathedral, which replaced the former mosque in the 15th century.

After you leave the vestibule, turn right along Alemanes, then right again at the end of the wall. Straight ahead is the Giralda, which you can now see full length. For a better look, bear left out into the middle of the:

3. **Plaza de la Virgen de los Reyes,** at the east end of the cathedral. The plaza and the ornate fountain in the middle benefited from a recent restoration, which included new paving stones. Presumably the café over at the corner of Calle Mateos Gago is once again allowed to set its tables out in the square. Face the entrance of the cathedral. The high square tower to the right is the:

4. **Giralda.** Now a campanile for the cathedral, it began life as the minaret for the mosque that once stood here. Its two architectural styles reflect both Moorish and Christian cultural elements. The lowest third, made of stone, was begun in 1182 under the caliphs of the Almohod dynasty; it is essentially plain. The middle third of the tower, however, is made of pale pink brick and decorated with a lacy lattice design, occasionally punctuated by pointed arches and horseshoe arches. The upper third was added in the 16th century, long after the Christians had seized Seville from the Moors. This section is lavishly embellished in high Renaissance style, with heavily carved balconies, sculptures, and a large chamber containing two dozen bells. At the very top is a bronze statue of an angel called Faith that rotates in the wind. (In Spanish, *giralda* means weathervane.) The tower is more than 320 feet tall. A ramp augmented by occasional stairs will take you to a platform near the top. It is a fairly easy climb, and you will be rewarded with spendid views of the city and river.

Next to the Giralda is the:

5. **Catedral,** its exterior bristling with spires and towers and the swoop of multiple flying buttresses. Begun in the early 15th century, it has both French Gothic and Renaissance design elements. The third largest cathedral in Europe (after St. Paul's in London and St. Peter's in Rome), it replaced a mosque that had served as a cathedral after the Moors were defeated in 1248. The interior is somewhat disappointing. Because large numbers of people came to the cathedral, an attempt was made to restrict their movement; thus, there is a perpetual gloom that keeps most of the chapels, choir, and high altar in murky shadow. The monster organ probably supplies the moments of highest drama when it rumbles to life.

It was here at this cathedral that the Infanta Elena, eldest daughter of King Juan Carlos and Queen Sofía, married Don Jaime de Marichalar in March 1995.

To the right of the cathedral, on the north side of the plaza, is an 18th-century archbishop's residence, which has an attractive Baroque doorway. Off to the left (south), you can glimpse the Alcázar. Turn around, and with your back to the cathedral, walk east on Calle Mateos Gago, past sidewalk cafés and souvenir and ceramic shops and beneath the orange trees that provide canopies over many of Seville's streets. Visitors are often tempted to pluck a dangling orange to eat, but few enjoy the experience since these oranges are very bitter. Sevillanos joke that since only the British can tolerate the taste, the harvests are shipped off to England. Actually this is the type of orange from which the British make their beloved marmalade.

After 2 blocks you will come to a building painted yellow ocher with white trim, a popular local color combination. On it are signs that read: *Colegio Público San Isidoro* and *Mesón del Moro.* Turn right, thereby entering the Barrio Santa Cruz. Immediately on your right is:

☕ **Take a Break** Pizzeria San Marco, Calle Mesón del Moro 6 (tel. 421-4390). This is one of a small chain of inexpensive restaurants specializing in pastas, individual pizzas, seafood dishes, and salads. You might want to return here later for lunch or dinner.

6. **Barrio Santa Cruz,** also known as **La Macarena.** Some of it dates back to the more tolerant period before the Inquisition, when it comprised the bustling Jewish quarter, the *Judería.* Most of the buildings you see here date from the 17th and 18th centuries, however, and the *barrio* is now a desirable residential neighborhood of whitewashed houses aligned along winding cobblestoned streets and picturesque plazas shaded by palms, bougainvillea, and citrus trees. Cars are banned from much of the area. Restaurants set tables outdoors beside bubbling fountains. Gated but open doorways invite visitors to peek in at tiled and planted inner courts. The romantic aura of the district is jarred occasionally by the insistent thump of rap music issuing from upstairs windows, but more often, the mood is enhanced

by strains of arias from *Carmen* or *Le Nozze di Figaro.* At night, in some of the *plazuelas,* young people sit about picking out flamenco tunes on their guitars.

Bear left at the end of the block, then turn immediately right onto Calle Santa Teresa. Throughout the area are a number of attractive little taverns, including **Taberna de Barrito,** at number 4. A little beyond, at number 8 is the **Casa-Museo Murillo,** one of several small galleries in a city that has only one midsize art museum. Casa-Museo Murillo is open Tuesday through Saturday from 10am to 2pm and 5 to 8pm, Sunday from 10am to 2pm.

The street soon opens onto the:

7. **Plaza Santa Cruz.** The small park in the center has a wrought-iron Victorian whimsy that incorporates the shapes of saints, winged creatures, and dragons to form a lamp and a cross. You might want to return to this attractive plaza for a couple of reasons. At the corner on the right is the best restaurant in the *barrio,* **La Albahaca,** at number 12, which is housed in a gracious old townhouse. Next to it, at number 11, is **Los Gallos,** one of only a few authentic flamenco clubs—called *tablaos*—in Seville. (Go after midnight, when aficionados outnumber tourists and the dancers have worked up a sweat.)

For now, however, bear right around the plaza, past the club, and turn right near a sign for the Hotel Murillo, quickly entering the Plaza Alfaro. Cross that square diagonally, heading toward the street at the opposite corner. Over to your left, tall trees mark the edge of the:

8. **Jardines de Murillo,** a park with extensive horticultural displays beneath spreading jacaranda and banyan trees. It is named for the painter, one of the city's favorite sons, who lived here from 1618 to 1682. Seville honors its artists more often than its generals—a reflection of its residents' priorities.

The street at the opposite corner is bordered by part of a newly restored fortification from the 8th and 9th centuries (the early years of the Moorish occupation). As you can see, pipes within the wall carried water to the original royal palace (on the site of today's Alcázar). Presumably, this is why the street is call *Agua* (water).

Those who own houses along the right side of the street lock their iron gates but usually leave the door open so that passersby can look into the patios and see their *azulejos* (glazed ceramic tiles) and luxuriant potted plants. The second building on the right has a plaque with a portrait of Washington Irving high up on the wall; the American author lived here in 1828 during his brief diplomatic career.

Turn right into the narrow alley, Justino de Neve, with its herringbone brick paving. This opens onto the:

9. **Plaza de los Venerables.** Straight ahead, at number 8, is the Hospital de Venerables Sacerdotes, which is now an art gallery. Even if the works on display there are not memorable, you might enjoy visiting the inner court, with its *azulejos* and robust orange trees. There is a modest entrance fee. A 17th-century chapel inside exhibits works by Valdés Leal, a local painter who was a contemporary of Murillo, although not as famous. The Hospital is open Tuesday through Sunday from 10am to 2pm and 4 to 8pm.

Plaza de los Venerables is one of the more commercialized plazas in the *barrio;* of its several taverns and restaurants, the most popular is the:

Take a Break Hostería del Laurel, Plaza de los Venerables 5 (tel. 422-0295). Small wooden tables and stools are arranged on the plaza near the entrance to the atmospheric bar, which is hung with whole hams and bundles of herbs. A small pitcher of sangría, the chilled Andalucian wine punch, and wedges of *tortilla,* a firm potato-and-egg omelet, are quite satisfying in this setting. The *hostería* also rents rooms and has a restaurant behind the bar.

Exit the plaza down the alley next to the Hospital's entrance, the one that has another restaurant, **Santa Cruz,** at the corner. This will soon bring you to the smaller:

10. **Plaza Doña Elvira,** which is also surrounded by orange trees with benches nestled beneath their branches. This square sometimes becomes a little bedraggled, especially after a typical weekend, when young people gather here to drink and play guitars.

Cross to the opposite corner, past the tables of another restaurant and up the alley called Calle Rodrigo Caro. This alley turns sharply left, then right, entering the much larger:

11. **Plaza de Alianza.** On the right are a café and a shop that sells tourist trinkets. Near the middle of the plaza is a dispirited fountain that is often out of order, and on the left is the continuing wall of the Alcázar. Across the plaza at the right corner is a shop called **Estudio John Fulton.** An American, Fulton came to Spain in the 1960s to learn how to be a matador. Despite the fact that non-Latin *toreros* have difficulty being accepted in the restricted world of bullfighting, he achieved a measure of success and stayed on to pursue a career as a painter, writer, and photographer. James Michener discussed Fulton at some length in his 1968 book *Iberia.*

After you pass the fountain, turn left and go down the wide set of stairs into Calle Joaquín Romero Murube. The Alcázar wall, now with the pointed crenellations typical of Moorish fortresses, angles here, too. On the right is a shop called **La Alcázaba,** at number 1. Many local stores sell ceramics with the delicate floral designs of the Sevillano style. This one sells only these ceramics and offers a large selection.

The next square is the:

12. **Plaza del Triunfo,** which adjoins the Plaza Virgen de los Reyes. The cathedral is now to your right. Continue straight ahead, keeping the Alcázar wall to your left. The wall soon cuts sharply left, descending to a massive portal with a ceramic lion above. That is the main entrance of the:

13. **Alcázar.** A Moorish palace occupied this site for a century or more before the Christian Reconquest of Seville in 1248. Only a few fragments of the former palace remain; they have been incorporated into this royal residence built between 1350 and 1369 for the Spanish king, Pedro the Cruel. He hired Muslim artisans to construct his Xanadu. The style is known as Mudejar. Although it made use of Moorish decorative elements, the materials and design were those preferred by the artisans' Christian employers. Although some of the Alcázar is closed to the public, you can

see courtyards layered in *azulejos* and intricately carved plasterwork that employs floral motifs and renderings of Arabic script. One wonders whether the Catholic monarchs who once lived here were aware that much of the stylized Arabic writing was offering praise to Allah.

Perhaps the most impressive chamber is the Salón de Embajadores (Hall of Ambassadors) with its splendid dome (requiring engineering technology not possessed by the Moors). As with the Alhambra, the reflecting pools encircled by columns that support scalloped arches are believed to evoke the desert oases of the Moors' ancestors. Below ground are vaulted baths that survived from the earlier Moorish structure. The self-guided tour passes through poorly tended gardens and apartments that were built for Carlos V in the 16th century. The Alcázar is open Tuesday through Saturday from 10:30am to 5pm, and Sundays and holidays from 10am to 1pm.

The customary route through the Alcázar exits onto the Plaza del Triunfo. Turn left, returning to the main entrance, and then turn right, walking along the south side of Calle Santo Tomás. Soon you will come to number 5 on the left, the:

14. **Museo de Arte Contemporaneo,** a small establishment with a broad interpretation of its mission. Included in its collection are folk costumes, furniture, housewares, farm tools, saddlery, and weapons. It's open to visitors, but the hours vary.

Across the street to the right is the:

15. **Casa Lonja,** a 16th-century financial exchange designed by Juan de Herrera (a royal favorite at that time). On the second floor, the building now houses a priceless collection of maps and documents dating from Spain's exploration and exploitation of the New World. Included are letters penned by Columbus and Magellan. The exhibits are rotated to minimize damage from light exposure, so it cannot be predicted what may be on view at any given time. The archives are open Monday through Saturday from 10am to 1pm.

Calle Santo Tomás ends at the Avenida de la Constitución, the most important downtown boulevard. Cross to the other side, turning left along the Avenida; you will soon arrive at a large traffic circle, the Plaza Fuerta de Jerez. At the next corner—marked by a perpetually busy bar/restaurant/sidewalk café—turn right on Calle Almirante Lobo. Cross the Paseo de Cristóbal Colón to the promenade that borders the Guadalquivir. The 12-sided tower that stands sentinel there is the:

16. **Torre del Oro** (Tower of Gold). Now its color is that of raw stone, but when built by the Moors in 1220, it was reputedly sheathed in gold-hued tiles that gleamed in the sun. There used to be a similar tower on the opposite side of the river with a heavy chain hung between them to prevent enemy ships from traveling up or down the river. The decorative battlements and balconies at the top were added in the 18th century. For a time, the tower was used as a prison, but now it houses a small maritime museum.

On the embankment below the tower several sightseeing river boats are moored. Turn right along the avenue and walk north. The pedestrian concourse has been substantially improved in recent years. Up ahead are a number of cafés with tables shaded by awnings; there is also a statue of Mozart holding a violin, in tribute to his operas that were set in Seville—*Don Giovanni* and *Le Nozze di Figaro*.

Appropriately, across the street, is the:

17. **Teatro de la Maestranza,** with a central cylindrical section and a separate facade of more traditional mien, painted in ocher and white. This is Seville's first true opera house, opened in 1992.

Continue along the promenade, now shaded by palms and flower-laden bushes. This is a favorite route of Sevillanos for their evening *paseo*—the traditional after-work, predinner constitutional. Two blocks from the opera house, on the same side of the boulevard, is the:

18. **Plaza de Toros de la Maestranza.** Whatever one's feelings about the spectacle that takes place within—the contest between man and bull with its inevitable end—this is a beautifully proportioned structure and probably the oldest in the world built for this purpose (1763).

Soon, on your left, you will come to a bridge that crosses the Guadalquivir, the:

Party Town

In a country that takes its celebrations seriously, Seville revels every spring in two that exemplify the Spanish penchant for juxtaposing the sacred and the secular and their superhuman capacity for squeezing the most from a 24-hour day.

The first celebration is *Semana Santa* (Holy Week), the week preceding Easter. Every *barrio* has a church, and each is supported by an organized brotherhood of devout parishioners called a *cofradía*. All 52 churches sponsor large floats known as *pasos,* with giant figures depicting the Virgin Mary or stages of the Passion of Christ. The figures, which may be 12 feet high, are made to look very real. The floats, which measure about 20 feet by 9 feet, may weigh up to half a ton each. They are carried on men's shoulders every night from Palm Sunday until the day before Easter. As many as 60 stevedores are required for each *paso,* and they work for up to 12 hours each night.

The floats—perhaps more accurately called "litters"— sway down narrow lanes and broad avenues to the coordinated roll of the shoulders of the stevedores. The processions are heralded by fife and drum corps, and onlookers often burst into a hoarse shout-song called *saeta.*

While robed *cofradías* lead the processions, the penitents bring up the rear. Barefoot, they either drag heavy chains or bear heavy crosses for 12 hours. The routes of the *pasos* are divided up so that each night there are only 9 to 12 different floats and their attendants.

The second spring celebration is the *Feria de Abril* (April Fair), which consists of bullfights, concerts, puppet shows, and other cheerful events to offset the solemnity of Holy Week.

Two thousand years ago, representatives of the Roman legions came to this place (called "Hispalis") to buy horses for their officers. The annual gathering grew, eventually attracting farmers, breeders, and buyers from distant districts of Iberia and even from France. Invariably the gathering attracted others who saw an opportunity to make a little money—Gypsy fortune-tellers, musicians, cooks, ironmongers, and artisans. Successful commerce was often celebrated around campfires at night; there were whole roasted pigs and lambs as well as wine and brandy.

Over the course of time, the commercial aspects of the gathering were minimized and the fun-filled events were maximized. Each spring now, a huge illuminated gateway is erected at the northern edge of a huge field on the western bank of the Guadalquivir. It attracts hundreds of thousands of Sevillanos and tens of thousands of visitors. Girls and women generally wear long tiered dresses with brightly colored ruffles and flounces, fringed shawls around their shoulders, and roses or carnations in their hair. Boys and men wear short snug jackets, flat-brimmed hats, and tooled leather chaps.

Families, unions, government agencies, businesses, and fraternal groups set up tents along temporary streets at the fairground. Called *casetas* (literally, "cottages"), the tents serve as temporary homes for the week. Some are simple, with dirt floors, rickety tables, and tinny boom boxes, while others are equipped with chandeliers, oil paintings, plush seating, and live orchestras.

Seville's aristocracy tends to celebrate by piling into ornate carriages drawn by teams of up to six horses with elaborate harnesses. Everyone stops at the *casetas* of friends to sip sherry and exchange the gossip of the fair.

Seville's dance is called the *sevillanas;* it is more graceful and rhythmic than flamenco but retains the sensuality of arched backs and flashing legs. At the *Feria,* tent flaps are drawn back, revealing scores of dazzling tableaux along each temporary street. Many of the *casetas* welcome strangers.

Arrangements to attend the *Semana Santa* or *Feria de Abril* must be made *at least* a year in advance. The prices of everything related to these events are extremely high. For lodgings, a good central source is Marketing Ahead, 433 Fifth Avenue, New York, NY 10016, an agency that represents Spain's nationwide *parador* chain, as well as many private hotels in the greater Seville region.

19. **Puente de Isabel II.** Go out on the bridge, perhaps pausing in the middle to watch people fishing from the banks,
and look at the river traffic, which includes foot-powered
paddle boats tracing lazy S-curves on the surface of the usually docile river. If you can plan to reach the bridge about
dusk, when the lights of the city are coming on, so much
the better. Most of the monuments are illuminated for a
few hours in the evening, and these can be seen to particular advantage from the west bank of the river. This is also
the hour of the first activity for creatures that flutter sound-
lessly around the bridge like swallows. They are bats, not
birds, but harmless.

At the other end of the bridge, take the first staircase
down to the left; it connects with Calle de Betís ("Betís"
was the Roman name for the river). This is perhaps the best
street on which to sample the *tapas* of Seville. Betís has more
than a dozen indoor taverns and the open-air bars called
chiringuitos between here and the next bridge. Several are
clustered at this end, and all have their specialities, with an
emphasis on seafood. Look for **Kiosko de las Flores,** with
many outdoor tables; **El Mero,** for fish fried in the airy
Málaga technique; **Los Maestrantes,** with its selection of
tempting cheeses and air-cured hams; **La Albaraza,** a wine
bar; and **Los Corritos,** an open-sided shed that looks temporary but has been around forever on the strength of its
tasty grilled sardines. Most of them are closed on Sunday.

Walk south, with the river on your left, and look at the
skyline on the opposite side. This section of the city, west
of Betís, is called **Triana.** A working-class district of
marginal touristic interest, it is often described as a Gypsy
neighborhood, but one really doesn't see too many
Gypsies here.

Toward the end of Betís, the bars, nightspots, and
restaurants increase in number once again. Over on the
left is:

Take a Break Río Grande, Betís 70 (tel. 427-3956)
The main attraction of this popular restaurant is its
unobstructed view of the Torre del Oro, the Giralda, the
boats gliding past, and the crowds of people coursing along
the opposite shore and across the nearby Puente San Telmo.
One can enjoy the view from the air-conditioned bar or

dining room, with their picture windows, or sit on the large terrace, at a table exposed to the sun or under an umbrella. It's open year round for much of the day and evening.

From the restaurant, turn left and cross the Puente San Telmo. When you reach the other side, cross what is here called the Avenida de las Delicias.

If it is dark at this time, it might be best to end your walk here since the rest of this tour will take you to areas where few people walk at night. Unfortunately, street crime has been increasing recently in Seville. During the day, however, there shouldn't be any problem.

To continue, walk straight ahead along the right side of Avenida G. Sanjurjo, which returns to the Puerta de Jerez. Stay on the south side of the circle and pick up Calle San Fernando. The building at the corner is the imposing:

20. **Hotel Alfonso XIII.** Originally built for the Ibero-American Fair in 1929 in mock Mudejar style, the hotel was thoroughly overhauled, inside and out, for Expo '92. It is still a prime gathering spot for Seville society, especially for predinner drinks around the inner court, and socially prominent people often choose to be married here. When the Infanta Elena, the eldest royal daughter, married Don Jaime de Marichalar at the Seville Cathedral in March 1995, their guests stayed here.

Continue down San Fernando. After you pass the hotel, the next building on the right is the:

21. **University.** It would be difficult to imagine the original function of this grandly proportioned 18th-century Baroque edifice, with its impressive dimensions, statuary, and courtyards. The truth is that this was a *fábrica de tabacos* (tobacco factory).

Continue down San Fernando to the next major intersection, Plaza de Don Juan de Austria. Turn right, along Avenida del Cid, walking 1 long block to another intersection, the Glorieta San Diego. Cross Palos de la Frontera, then bear left across what is now called the Avenida de Maria Luisa, and finally turn down the diagonal Avenida Isabel la Católica. This street enters the Parque de María Luisa, with its towering trees and wide lawns, that was formerly the private grounds of the Palacio San Telmo.

After Expo

As Barcelona did with its upcoming Olympics, Seville did with its approaching world's fair (Expo) in 1992; it modernized its infrastructure. With the sympathetic support of Prime Minister González (a Sevillano), a new railbed and high-speed train called the AVE reduced the travel time between Madrid and Seville from more than 7 hours to just 2½. A new train station, Santa Justa, was constructed and the airport was upgraded.

Expo itself was erected on the island of Cartuja, in the middle of the river. Cable cars carried visitors between the island and the city, and six bridges were added. Cartuja, which had little except an ancient monastery before the fair, now boasts a five-star hotel and almost 50 pavilions left over from Expo. They have been converted to other uses, such as a 173-acre theme park. The operators of the park claimed that there were more than 4 million visitors during its first year. The park hosts circuses, flamenco *tablaos,* classical and rock concerts, cafés, and outdoor movies.

Although Seville is the setting for at least 20 operas, the city had no suitable performance hall until April 1992, with the opening of the Teatro de la Maestranza. Now Carmen, Don Juan, and The Barber have a proper setting in which to express their loves and laments.

Since Expo, another artistic deficiency has been remedied. The Museo de Bellas Artes enjoyed a triumphant reinauguration in April 1993. Founded in 1835 (in a 17th-century convent building), the museum had experienced many failed attempts at expansion and renovation over the years. But now the collection of paintings by such masters as Velázquez and Murillo are once again on view, along with works by El Greco and Goya. The principal display area is the former convent's chapel, perhaps a fitting circumstance since much of the collection was confiscated from monasteries and churches during the 19th-century anticlerical period. The museum is at Plaza del Museo 9 and is open Tuesday through Sunday from 9am to 3pm.

To your left, you can see part of another structure, the:

22. **Plaza de España.** During the 1929 Ibero-American Fair (a trade fair), this was a center of activity. The building curves in a giant semicircle and the broad plaza in front is bounded on the other side by a half-moon canal. The bridges over the canal seem to require constant tile repair, but they lend a romantic quality to the complex. Wedding parties often come here to pose for photographs, horse-drawn carriages regularly stop here, and one can rent rowboats for the canal that goes nowhere. All in all, a pleasant way to end your introduction to this most Spanish of Spanish cities.

SALAMANCA

Start: Plaza Mayor.

Finish: Plaza Mayor.

Time: 2 to 3 hours, not including rest stops.

Best Times: Any day from 9am to 7pm.

Worst Times: Winter evenings after 5pm.

Many Spanish towns and a few small cities look as if they erupted whole from beneath the earth's surface. This is because their builders worked with what they found at their feet. In a nation denuded of much of its former forest cover, that meant stone, not wood or brick or shingles. In Salamanca, the color of that stone is honey or gold or even permutations of pink or rose depending on time of day and weather conditions.

After forming your first impression, much of your pleasure in strolling through Salamanca will be in observing the details. The old city is compact and roughly oval, and every block seems to have a significant church, palace, college, or mansion. Most of them date from the early 16th century, when the mature Gothic and young Renaissance architectural styles converged.

Two submovements bridged that transition in many parts of Spain but especially in Salamanca. Concurrent with the reign of Isabel and Fernando, and especially after the voyage of Columbus and the capture of the last Moorish stronghold on the peninsula, a decorative style emerged that was called "Isabeline." It consisted of painstakingly carved stone, much of it reminiscent of the sinuous Arabic script that covered the walls of captured Moorish palaces but also including carefully rendered escutcheons, busts of notables, real and mythical animals, and twirls and curlicues of floral vegetation.

That style segued into a still more lavish form called "Plateresque," because it resembled the delicate complexity of the silverwork of the time (*Plata* is "silver" in Spanish). In addition to the influence of Isabeline style, Plateresque included Italian elements, and some of the artisans who worked with the Plateresque style were Italian.

Salamanca was also home to three Churriguera brothers, who lived from the late 17th century into the 18th. Their lush, sumptuous ornamentation, a Spanish variation of the Baroque, took its cue from the Isabeline and Plateresque of a century earlier. Most of their work is found inside churches and palaces.

Intricate stone carving probably flourished in Salamanca because of its native sandstone. When first quarried, this sandstone is highly malleable and accepting of the carver's chisel, especially after repeated soaking with water.

• • • • • • • • • • • • • • • •

To begin this tour, go to the middle of:

1. **Plaza Mayor,** a gift of Felipe V to express his gratitude to the Salmantinos for their support during the War of the Spanish Succession. Early in the 18th century, that conflict involved a number of European powers all of which wanted to place their own candidates on the Spanish throne to replace the last Hapsburg monarch. Suffice it to say that Felipe, the first Bourbon King, claimed the throne and survived the ensuing 14 years of battle. This plaza is not only the finest enclosed square in Spain but also rivals in its quiet grandeur any English, French, or Italian plaza.

An arcade of 88 rounded arches extends around all four sides and is surmounted by three floors with balustraded, shuttered windows. If you examine them closely, you will see that the arches are not uniform, but the effect vaguely resembles the gently wavering lines on the columns of the Parthenon. Six porticos are evenly spaced leading to the streets that radiate out from the plaza. The only interruptions in the overall symmetry are, on the north side, the *Ayuntamiento* (city hall), which protrudes importantly into the square, and, on the east, the roof comb of the Royal Pavilion, which bears a depiction of Felipe, the benefactor. It was he who hired the Churriguera brothers, who became famous for a florid Baroque decoration that is named for them. The plaza was begun in 1729 and finished in 1755.

Between the arches on two of the four facades are medallions in relief honoring such noted nationals as El Cid, Pizarro, Isabel, Fernando, and Juana the Mad. One medallion, routinely defaced, often by insulting splashes of red paint, is of Generalissimo Franco, Spain's dictator from the end of the Civil War in 1939 until his death in 1975.

For the past couple of decades the plaza has been free of vehicular traffic except for police cars and delivery vans. About a dozen cafés and restaurants beneath the arcades now set out tables and chairs whenever the weather permits, attracting students, lovers, families, and tourists from breakfast until after midnight. The plaza is frequented by Salmantinos, whether to cross it, to meet friends, or simply just to *be* there.

Exit the plaza by the northwest corner, into Calle del Concejo. After you pass the Plaza de la Libertad, you will soon reach the:

2. **Plaza de los Bandos,** a park bounded on the far side by the Palacio Garci Grande and on the left by the Iglesia Nuestra Señora del Carmen. Walk past the front of the church; at that corner is the:

3. **Casa de Dama María la Brava,** with a 15th-century coat of arms. It is now a college of pharmacy, one of many university buildings scattered around the old quarter.

Turn left down the narrow lane between the college and the church, Calle Espoz y Mina. At the next corner, turn right on Cuesta del Carmen. After 2 blocks, turn left on Calle Bordadores. There is no sign at that point, but the street leads to a triangular plaza on the right, bordered by the eastern end of the:

Salamanca

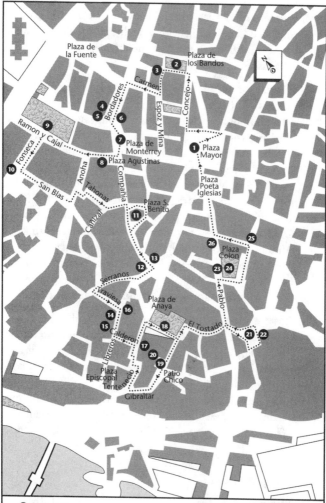

1. Plaza Mayor
2. Plaza de los Bandos
3. Casa de Dama María la Brava
4. Convento las Ursulas
5. Statue of Miguel de Unamuno
6. Casa de las Muertes
7. Plaza de Monterrey
8. Iglesia de la Purisima
9. Paseo Campo de San Francisco
10. Colegio del Arzobispo Fonseca
11. Iglesia San Benito
12. Clerecia
13. Casa de las Conchas
14. Patio de las Escuelas
15. Escuelas Menores
16. University
17. Catedral Nueva
18. Plaza de Anaya
19. Patio Chico
20. Catedral Vieja
21. Plaza de Santo Domingo
22. Convento de San Esteban
23. Palacio de Orellana
24. Plaza de Colón
25. Torre del Clavero
26. Palacio de Fonseca

4. **Convento las Ursulas,** a convent that dates in part to the 15th century but with a 16th-century church and a museum that are open to the public. In middle of the small plaza is a:

5. **Statue of Miguel de Unamuno,** an intellectual hero of Spain but especially of Salamanca. A novelist, essayist, and philosopher, Unamuno was a professor of Greek at the University of Salamanca when Miguel Primo de Rivera became dictator in 1923. Unamuno's criticism of the monarchy and military government led to his dismissal from the university and his exile from Spain until the emergence of the fragile Second Republic in 1930. Unamuno was installed as rector of the university in 1931 and mildly supported the democratic experiment. Although he sided briefly with Franco's nationalist Rebels at the outbreak of the Civil War, he later condemned them as well.

Unamuno's statue glowers across the street at the:

6. **Casa de las Muertes** (House of the Dead). The reason for its name is immediately apparent. Commissioned by Archbishop Fonseca in the mid-16th century, its facade has four skulls under the two windows on the top floor. However, the building is better known for its Plateresque decoration, consisting of floral motifs, angels standing on dolphins, peacocks, and busts of Fonseca and members of his family. Unamuno died in the house next door (number 4) in 1936.

Continue in the same direction—the street is now called Compañia—until you reach the:

7. **Plaza de Monterrey,** which is named for the Palacio de Monterrey over on your right. Begun in 1539, it had a square tower that presumably was used for defensive purposes. Turn right at the palacio and enter the Plazuela de las Augustinas. On your left is the:

8. **Iglesia de la Purisima,** begun in 1636. The church has a painting of the Immaculate Conception by Ribera installed above the high altar. Ordered built by a viceroy of Naples, the Count of Monterrey, the church has Italianate elements on both its exterior and interior.

"Long Live Death"

By the last year of his life, Miguel de Unamuno had become frail, due in large measure to his duties as rector of the university and his role as one of the country's leading intellectuals at a time of harrowing conflict. By October 12, 1936, Salamanca was under the firm control of the Rebel Falangists. On that day, a group of clergymen, dignitaries, victorious generals, and even Franco's wife met in an ancient lecture hall of the university. It was El Día de la Raza (the Day of the Race) a traditional time to commemorate the voyages of Columbus. One of the generals was the one-eyed, one-armed José Millán Astray. Perhaps his many battle wounds, sustained in mostly unsuccessful campaigns in Morocco, loosened his grip on reality and logic. In any event, the general leapt to his feet, interrupting the proceeding, and launched a lengthy and probably psychotic condemnation of learning, books, universities, and intellectuals.

"Long live death!" he cried. "Down with intelligence!"

Although one cannot reason with someone who expresses such sentiments, Unamuno tried. By most accounts, Unamuno was gentle in his attempts to do so, but these efforts only provoked the general into shrieks of rage. Surrounded by Franco's soldiers and police, Unamuno was ushered out of the lecture hall and placed under house arrest. He died shortly thereafter.

Proceed along Calle Ramón y Cajal, which leads past a church with a heavily embellished portal. Half a block farther, there is a break in the wall on the right, allowing you to enter:

9. **Paseo Campo de San Francisco,** a semiformal park with many places where you can sit for a while in the shade of towering primeval trees.

   Exit the park where you entered and proceed straight into Calle Fonseca. The long building on your right is the:

10. **Colegio del Arzobispo Fonseca,** which dates from 1521. Later in that century, it became a college for training Irish

priests and is also known as Colegio de los Irlandeses. Seminarians were required to undergo 8 years of rigorous study. The college continued to train priests into the mid-20th century but has now become a school of social sciences and communications of the University of Salamanca. The building is open daily from 9am to 2pm and 4 to 7pm. Inexpensive tickets can be purchased from the attendant in the office inside to the left. Then walk straight ahead into the graceful Renaissance courtyard. Over to the right, a glass window has been installed to reveal an unusual spiral staircase, made entirely of stone, that seems to float without support. When you return to the vestibule, you will see the entrance to the chapel. Inside there is a striking retable with paintings, sculptures, and decorative flourishes. Some of this was executed by Alfonso Berruguete, a prominent 16th-century sculptor who studied for a time in Italy and was deeply influenced by the work of Michelangelo.

After you exit the Colegio, cross over and continue down the opposite street, Cuesta de San Blas, passing a small church on the right. Up ahead, you can see the domes and spires of the monumental heart of Salamanca. At the bottom of the hill, turn left a few steps on Calle Ancha, then immediately right on Tahonas Viejas. At the end, turn left on Cañizal. This street ends at Compañia.

Straight ahead is the back of:

11. **Iglesia San Benito,** a late 15th-century church that is still being restored. Go around to the front to view its Gothic-Isabeline facade. The houses close by were once owned by the aristocratic families that formed the contentious *bandos* of the time. Many of them, too, are being renovated. Prominent among them, on the left, is the Casa de Maldonado Rivas, which belonged to one of the most powerful families. They held proprietary influence over the church and the *barrio*.

After you go around the church, turn left on Compañia. Dominating the opposite side of the street is the:

12. **Clerecia,** a Jesuit seminary begun in the early 17th Century and recently reopened after extensive renovations.

The star attraction on this street, however—just across Compañia—is the:

13. **Casa de las Conchas,** one of the most photographed buildings in Salamanca. Completed in 1483 for a member of one of the city's powerful Renaissance families, the facade is notable for its 16 even rows of 400 scallop shells sculpted in stone. Talavera Maldonado was a knight in the Order of Santiago (St. James), the most prominent figure in the national canon. The symbol of Santiago was the scallop shell (*concha*). In Galicia, where he is alleged to be buried, pilgrims to his tomb wear the shells and many rural homes are covered in whole or in part with them. The Isabeline windows are equally appealing. After years of restoration work, the mansion has been reopened as a library. Step inside to see the patio, including the carved lion heads at the top of the columns of the ground floor loggia. Each head is different and holds in its mouth a large ring bearing a heraldic shield. Above the lion heads are gargoyles that function as rainspouts.

After you leave the mansion, turn left into Compañia and then right onto Rua Antigua (alongside the Clerecia), which soon becomes Calle de Serranos. Soon, on the left, you will come to:

Take a Break   Café Bar Mandela, Calle de Serranos 9–11 (tel. 12-33-42). You will find tantalizing displays of *tapas,* sandwiches, tarts, and cakes displayed at the bar to the right of the entrance. This establishment is popular with students and young families; there are additional tables upstairs to accommodate the overflow. Current pop and alternative rock are played at tolerable levels on the stereo. Open daily from 7:30am to 1am.

When you exit the café, continue to the next corner and turn left on Calle Traviesa for 1 block; turn right, then right again into the courtyard called:

14. **Patio de las Escuelas** (Schools' Square). Circle the patio, ignoring, for the moment, the striking building that faces the open end. The statue in the center is of Luis de Ponce de León, a monk and professor of theology at the university.

The wall to the left (south) has two Plateresque doorways, the first leading into a 1533 student infirmary and the second to:

Friar Detained

In 1492 Spanish Jews were ordered to make a choice: convert to Catholicism or leave the country. Ten years later, a similar edict was issued to resident Muslims. The infamous Inquisition had begun, and anyone who could be viewed as a heretic was in danger for the next three centuries. In due time, accusatory fingers pointed at the University of Salamanca, which was in large part a school of theology. In 1573, Fray Luis de León came under suspicion. A poet and teacher of considerable fame, Fray Luis was an avid biblical scholar. He translated the "Song of Songs" into Spanish—one of his notable achievements, until critics claimed he was exalting Judaism, the banned faith. The friar was thrown into prison and kept there almost 5 years while being tried intermittently for unspecified transgressions brought by unidentified accusers. Finally, he was released and returned to his lecture hall at the university. Mounting his podium, he looked around at his students and colleagues, some of whom were probably responsible for having him jailed. Finally he intoned, "Dicebamus hesterna die. . . . " ("As we were saying yesterday. . . . ")

15. **Escuelas Menores** (Lower School) or college preparatory institutes. What you see is a double-arched door enclosed by a larger rounded arch. Up above, the largest of the three shields is that of Carlos V, who was the King of Spain and Holy Roman Emperor during the first half of the 16th century. At the roofline is a virtual tiara (or comb) of stone. Step inside for a glance around the 1428 Gothic patio. In the far corner is a similarly impressive Renaissance portal to what is now the University Museum.

   Return to the open end of the courtyard and look at facade of the:

16. **University,** which rises five stories high. The building, completed in 1433, is Gothic, but its most striking feature is the glorious Plateresque facade, which was added in 1529. The riotous details of the carved front are as sharply

defined today as 450 years ago. Among the entwined motifs are double-headed eagles of the Hapsburg dynasty,
cupids, mythical animals and gods, sinuous vines and leaves,
and busts of well-known personages (including Isabel and
Femando) framed by scallop shells and medallions. A Greek
inscription reads: "The Monarchs for the University and
the University for the Monarchs."

Somewhere in that carved extravaganza is a frog—*una
rana*—no bigger than a toddler's fist. Anyone who can find
the frog without assistance is supposed to be guaranteed
good luck. If you would like to look for it for yourself, do
so now (the answer will be found below).*

Inside, over to the left of the central courtyard, is the
classroom of Fray Luis de León. It has been left as it was
when he finished teaching in the 16th century. Desks and
benches for students are no more than logs with a very narrow flattened side. Spending an hour on them was surely
excruciating, especially when combined with the often frigid
winter mornings. Actually, they were a step up in comfort,
since most lecture halls at that time had no seating whatever. Students stood or sat on the floor. At the front is the
lectern used by Fray Luis.

As you leave the university, turn left, then left again on
Calderón de la Barca. Up ahead, framed between houses
on either side, is a portal and tower of the so-called:

17. **Catedral Nueva** (New Cathedral). Construction of this
cathedral began in 1513 and was essentially completed
within 50 years, although additions and modifications
continued for another two centuries. It is called "New
Cathedral" since it abuts an older cathedral dating from
the 12th century. Although this facade incorporates
Romanesque and Renaissance elements, it is essentially
late Gothic. It may not *look* Gothic, however, since it was
constructed of wheat-colored sandstome and its sculptural
details are as sharply incised as when they left the

Answer: Look at the vertical column that rises from the right of the doors
to the top of the facade. About one third of the way up are three skulls
looking down at the street. The one on the left has a tiny frog (probably
toad) clinging to its forehead, which is supposed to represent sin. If it
still eludes you, perhaps one of the other onlookers will be able to point
it out.

stonecutter's workshop. Before you enter the cathedral, walk along to the left. Notice the abundance of detail around this door and the one next to it. Look for the unicorn, the apeman, the walking fish, the manatee, the headless Roman senator, the mother owl and her two offspring, the baby elephant, the cocker spaniel, cats, and occasionally a well-endowed nude man—all disguised by the voluptuous branches and leaves of stone vines. Walk along to the left and shortly you will emerge into the:

18. **Plaza de Anaya,** which has a formal grove of trees at the center and four rectangular patches of grass. Up on the wall to the left is a tablet that quotes from Cervantes: "Salamanca casts a spell on those who have enjoyed the peacefulness of life here, awakening the desire to return." On the opposite side of the plaza is the neoclassical Palacio de Anaya, begun in 1760 and now a college of the university. It adjoins the Baroque church of San Sebastián, designed by Alberto Churriguera and completed in 1731.

    Stay on the cathedral side of the square and approach the church doorway immediately on your right. Although it is lavishly embellished, you will notice that the stone near the bottom of the frame is of a different color, indicating that repairs have been made recently. New figures and creatures have been incorporated into the design. Starting at the right doorframe and going to the left, you should be able to identify a large cricket, a bull, a troll, a stork, a rabbit and . . . an astronaut. Yes, an astronaut, floating in space, his umbilical cord trailing out behind him.

    Continue down through the plaza, bearing right after reaching the east end of the cathedral. This street shortly emerges into:

19. **Patio Chico,** and to the right you can now see the Cathedral Vieja. Since its tiled conical tower once bore a rooster weathervane, it is called *Torre del Gallo*. Reportedly the Old Cathedral was in danger of collapsing during the 16th century. Instead of razing it, however, the New Cathedral was built up against it to provide support. Thus the older structure was saved—a rare example of enlightened preservation. Compare the simple rounded arches and flat buttresses of the Old Cathedral with the florid excesses of its younger Gothic neighbor.

Continue through Patio Chico, bearing right on Calle Gibraltar and then right again onto Calle Tentenecio. This rises into the Plaza Episcopal. On your left is a former bishop's residence that became Franco's headquarters during the Civil War; it now serves as a municipal museum and archive. Continue to the door of the New Cathedral on your right and enter. Both cathedrals are open from 10am to 1pm and 4 to 6pm October to March, and from 10am to 2pm and 4 to 8pm April through September.

Within the New Cathedral the stalls in the *coro* (the chancel in the middle of the nave) were designed by Alberto Churriguera, and the wall surrounding the *coro* was the work of his brother Joaquin.

To the right inside the front door of the New Cathedral is the entrance to the:

20. **Cathedral Vieja.** Many visitors prefer the stolid simplicity of this Romanesque church to the busy flamboyance of its sibling. It is an antidote to the surfeit of Gothic churches encountered on a European visit. The relatively compact spaces were intended, not to humble the worshiper, but to facilitate communion with God. The church was completed around 1190, toward the end of the Romanesque vogue, when architects were beginning to discover how to make churches taller, wider, and more spacious. That's why the traditional rounded arches have begun to show rudimentary points at the top, leading to the subsequent Gothic style. Much of the carved stonework was painted (like classical Greek statuary) and traces of color remain.

Leave by the main door of the New Cathedral and turn right, returning to the Plaza de Anaya. Continue through the plaza, past the Palacio de Amaya and into the narrow Calle el Tostado. This angles around to the left and merges into Calle San Pablo. Stay to the right as you enter:

21. **Plaza de Santo Domingo;** on the left you will see the **Convento de Santa Maria de las Dueñas,** a still-active Dominican convent. Its remarkable 16th-century Renaissance cloister is open to the public from 10:30am to 1pm and 4 to 5:30pm October through March, and from 10am to 1pm and 4 to 7pm April through September. Beyond the convent, somewhat to the right, is a short footbridge that leads to the:

22. **Convento de San Esteban.** The convent church, which attracts many visitors, is essentially late Gothic but with a Plateresque west facade of exquisite complexity. By emphasizing the stoning of San Esteban (St. Stephen), the Italian sculptor had an opportunity to create a scene with multitudes of people and prancing horses. Inside is a retable designed by José Churriguera. Off to the right, through a portico with ten arches, is the cloister. Columbus stayed in one of its cells when he came to Salamanca seeking support for his proposed voyage.

     Return to San Pablo and turn right, up the hill. At the next corner on your left, Calle Palominos, look at the steeples of the Clerecia. At the next corner, also on your left, is the:

23. **Palacio de Orellana,** a mansion that is interesting primarily because it was built during the early 17th century—the transitional period between the end of the Renaissance and the blossoming of the Baroque. On the third floor is an open gallery adjoining a tower. To the right is the park-like:

24. **Plaza de Colón.** In the middle is a statue of Columbus pointing west, to the New World. Turn right, walking along the south side, toward the small **Iglesia de San Pablo.** The church is worth approaching because of the unusual noise arising from its roof. Visitors to many towns in this region of Spain (western Castile bordering Portugal) often hear periodic eruptions of hollow clacking, somewhat like two halves of a length of hollow bamboo being clapped together. The sound rises in a crescendo, suddenly trailing off, and is usually answered by a similar racket. The noise is made by a group of storks on the top of this small church's bell tower. They make the arrhythmic noise by slapping their long bills together. You can approach and observe these particular storks more closely than most. When startled, they will lift off and glide away in a graceful manner; they are snowy white except for the bands of black feathers along the trailing edges of their powerful wings.

     Turn left in front of the church. Up ahead, at the northeast corner of the plaza, is the 15th-century:

25. **Torre del Clavero,** with eight small sentry turrets. This is all that survives of a castle that once stood here. It now houses a small municipal museum.

Turn left along the "top" of the plaza, then right into San Pablo. On the left is the:

26. **Palacio de Fonseca,** built for this prominent family in the mid-16th century and now housing government offices. Beyond the high iron gate is a patio with a cantilevered upper gallery that merits a brief look.

Proceed along San Pablo. Soon, on the right, you will come to Plaza del Peso, which is actually just a side street. Over on the left, down a short flight of stairs, is:

Take a Break Rio de la Plata, Plaza del Peso 1 (tel. 21-90-05). At the back is one of the best dining rooms in Salamanca. Up front at the bar are platters of raw ingredients for *tapas,* most of which are prepared to order, rather than precooked and warmed-up. Plaques and certificates on the walls attest to the kitchen's gastronomic prowess. You could have lunch or dinner here, or else just a drink and a snack. Open from noon to 11pm Tuesday through Sunday, it is closed in July. No credit cards.

To return to Plaza Mayor, backtrack to San Pablo and cross the Plaza Poeta Iglesias. Over to your right is the recently renovated Gran Hotel. Walk through the entrance straight ahead into the Plaza Mayor. Activity will probably be picking up if the workday is over and the evening *paseo* has begun.

It may require a little aggressiveness to snare a seat at one of the cafés, but it will be worth it, just to enjoy the parade. If you are lucky, there will be fiestas, singing groups, or even fireworks, if a fiesta is on. Some nights, a stage is set up for a rock concert. Almost every night, student singing groups called *tunas* meander from bar to bar. Dressed in the velvets and capes of medieval troubadours, they sing traditional songs, accompanying themselves with guitars, mandolins, and tambourines. Gratuities are accepted. *Tunas* are all found all over Spain, but nowhere do they seem more fitting than here, in the gathering Salamanca night.

ESSENTIALS & RECOMMENDED READING

BARCELONA

Capital of the four-province region of Catalunya ("Cataluña" in Spanish, "Catalonia" in English), Barcelona is the second-largest city on the Iberian Peninsula, with a population of more than 1,700,000. Situated on the Mediterranean Sea in the northeastern section of Spain, most of its major sights are located in and near the old city—Ciutat Vella—at the edge of the largely man-made harbor and on adjacent Montjuïc Hill. The Plaça de Catalunya is centrally located between Ciutat Vella and the 19th-century expansion district, Eixample. It is served by bus and subway lines from outer neighborhoods, by El Prat airport, and by railroads from Madrid and France.

Getting There

By Plane   Expanded and modernized El Prat Airport is about 8 miles from downtown, with a convenient railway connection from the terminal. Iberia and TWA have nonstop flights to Barcelona from New York, and Delta flies there nonstop from Atlanta at least three times a week. There is an hourly air shuttle called the Puente Aereo ("Air Bridge") that connects Madrid and Barcelona. Call Iberia (tel. 93/401-3131) at the airport for details and reservations.

By Train   RENFE, the Spanish national railway, has several trains daily from Madrid and other Spanish cities. Nearly all of them stop at Estació Sants (tel. 93/490-0202), and some continue to an underground station on Passeig de Gràcia, near the Plaça de Catalunya. Trains from France stop at the refurbished Estació de França near the site of the 1992 Olympic Village. The fastest trains are called *talgos;* those labeled *rápido* are badly misnamed. It is best to buy your ticket through a travel agency, since ticket-sellers at railroad stations seldom speak English.

By Bus   An extensive network of bus routes reaches into every corner of Spain, with frequent connections between Barcelona and other cities. For distances of 250 miles or less, buses are often cheaper and faster than trains. They are run by private companies, and the coaches range from very comfortable, with reclining seats, stereo, and TV, to strictly utilitarian with little legroom. There is no reliable way to know in advance which type of bus you will encounter. Most buses arrive and leave from the Estació del Nord (tel. 93/245-2528), two blocks east of the Passeig de Sant Joan, at the corner of Avinguda de Vilanova and Carrer de Nàpolis.

By Car   *Autopistas*—toll highways—run down to Barcelona from the French border at Portbou (less than 2 hours' travel time) and along the east coast from Valencia (less than 4 hours). The *autopistas* from Madrid to Barcelona are less direct, running northeast to Zaragoza, then east through Lleida (requiring about 7 hours). Tolls are higher than those usually charged in North America.

Getting Around

Saving Money   A transportation card, good for 10 trips, will help you to economize. The **Tarjeta T-1** is good for the Metro,

Barcelona Metro

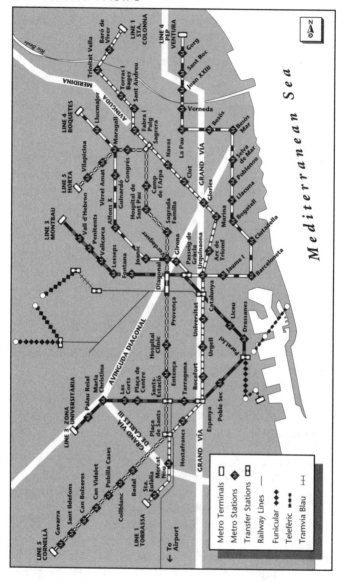

bus, Montjuïc funicular, and Tramvía Blau. There are also **three-day passes** and **five-day passes,** which enable you to ride as often as you want on both the Metro and city buses. A helpful publication is the *Guía del Transport Públic,* which is available free at most tourist offices or at the office of **Transports**

Metropolita de Barcelona, Plaça de Catalunya, open Monday to Friday from 8am to 7pm and Saturday from 8am to 1pm.

By Subway   Barcelona's metro system is made up of five main lines that cover most of the city more quickly and efficiently that the city's buses. The major station is the centrally located Plaça de Catalunya. Trains run Monday to Friday from 5am to 11pm, Saturday from 5am to 1am, and Sunday and holidays from 6am to 1am.

By Bus   Although there are about 50 bus lines that cover the city, it is best to avoid them during rush hours. Most buses operate daily from 6:30am to 10pm; some night buses use the city's major boulevards between 10pm and 4am. The red buses are daytime buses that operate in the city center and stop at major squares, while the blue ones are nighttime buses.

By Taxi   Taxis are yellow-and-black. If you see a lit green light on the roof and a *Libre* or *Lliure* ("free") sign in the window, you will know that the taxi is available. *Note:* When you get into a taxi, make sure that the driver begins the meter at the initial rate (some drivers may not set the meter at all or may not turn it back after the last passenger left the taxi). There are legitimate surcharges for "special situations" such as driving to the airport, transporting a large suitcase, or riding at night or on Saturday, Sunday, and holidays.

To call a cab, dial 330-0804, 300-3811, or 358-1111.

MADRID

All roads lead to Madrid, as was planned by the monarchs who made it the capital of a country of fractious regions. At the approximate geographic center of the peninsula, Central Madrid's population is about 3,100,000. New ring roads enable one to bypass much of the city's worst traffic; there are several important boulevards running both north and south and east and west through the city. Madrid is a relatively "new" city, making it easier to negotiate than many other Spanish cities, except for the older section around the plaza Puerta del Sol. Comprehensive networks of metro and bus lines extend out from that central point to all corners of the city, but especially into the newer northern sections that have been developed in the decades since the Civil War.

Madrid Metro

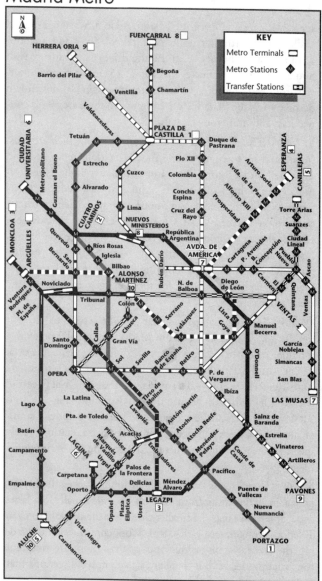

KEY

Metro Terminals ▭
Metro Stations ◆
Transfer Stations ▭

Getting There

By Plane   Iberia, the Spanish national airline, has daily flights from New York to Madrid and, less regularly, from other North American cities. Reciprocal agreements allow TWA, Continental, American, United, and Delta to fly nonstop to Madrid from several U.S. cities: New York, Miami, Atlanta, Washington, and Dallas-Fort Worth. Barajas Airport (tel. 91/305-8343) is about 7 miles east of the city, a 20-minute drive except during rush hours. A shuttle bus makes that trip at 15- to 30-minute intervals from early morning to well after midnight. Its downtown destination is the Plaza Colón, from which there are metro connections and numerous taxicabs.

By Train   There are three train stations, two of which are most frequented by foreign visitors. Atocha Station, renovated and expanded into a tourist destination in its own right, is the terminal for the high-speed AVE trains that have reduced travel time to Seville from more than 7 hours to only $2^1/_2$. It also handles trains to the southern coast. Chamartín Station, at the northern edge of the city, accommodates trains from France, Barcelona, Lisbon, and other points north. The Norte Station is primarily for commuter trains. When buying your ticket for trains other than the excellent AVE, ask for those designated as *talgos,* the next fastest category.

By Bus   The bus companies that provide service to cities at middle and long distances from Madrid are usually preferable for rides of up to 2 hours (such as to Toledo, Avila, Segovia, Cuenca, and Salamanca). The most important bus stations are Auto-Rés (tel. 91/551-7200) at Plaza Conde de Casal 6, east of the Atocha railroad terminal, and Estación del Sur (tel. 91/468-4200) at Calle Canarias 17, about 6 blocks south of the same terminal. Since ticket-sellers at bus stations rarely speak English, it might be better to buy your ticket through a travel agent.

By Car   Good roads, most of them limited-access highways, radiate in all directions from Madrid. They are usually four lanes wide, at least as far as the smaller cities near the capital: Segovia, Toledo, Chincón, and El Escorial. Work continues on upgrading the road system, which means that there are frequent construction delays, but there are also completed sections that may appear to be unfinished even on recent maps.

Getting Around

By Subway   The metro system is relative easy to learn, since all lines converge at Puerta del Sol. Although the metro operates from 6am to 1:30am, it is best to avoid the rush hours. For information, call 552-4900. You can save money on the metro by purchasing a 10-trip ticket known as a *bono.*

By Bus   There is a network of buses to serve both the city and its suburbs; their routes are clearly shown on a schematic diagram at each bus stop. Buses in Madrid are fairly fast and efficient because they have special lanes, thereby avoiding the usual congestion. You can also economize by purchasing a 10-trip bus ticket, although it cannot be used on transfers. The ticket is available at **Empresa Municipal de Transportes,** Plaza de la Cibeles (tel. 401-9900), whose office is open daily from 8am to 8:30pm; they also sell a bus route guide.

By Taxi   Cab fares, although they have risen lately, are still reasonably priced. *Note:* When you get into a cab, make sure that the driver turns the meter on; otherwise, he can charge you almost anything he chooses. The meter will register an initial rate; after that, you will be charged for each kilometer. There are legitimate surcharges for "special situations": a trip to the railway station, the airport, and to or from the bullring, as well as for riding on Sunday and holidays. If your trip entails going outside the city limits, the driver can double the fare. It's customary to tip at least 10% of the fare.

There are unmetered taxis; although they are legal, they have no meters and can charge higher rates. You can avoid them by looking for standard taxis—they are either black with horizontal red bands, or white with diagonal red bands.

To call a cab, dial 445-9008 or 447-5180.

GRANADA

Granada stands at the edge of a broad plain; its dramatic backdrop is the Sierra Nevada range, which is often snowcapped in June. With a current population of about 264,000, Granada has been the beneficiary of important infrastructural improvements in recent years, primarily bridges and ring roads. Most tourists want to focus on the Alhambra, the complex of palaces and gardens covering a ridge above the city. Several hotels and hostels in varying price ranges are located on the Alhambra grounds, but most accommodations and restaurants are in the newer city below. Access to the Alhambra is by car, bus, or on foot.

Getting There

By Plane Aviaco, a domestic feeder airline, has daily flights to and from Madrid and Barcelona and less frequent connections with other cities. The airport (tel. 958/44-64-11) is about 11 miles from downtown Granada. Buses connect the airport with the Plaza Isabel la Católica, about a 20-minute ride during nonrush hours.

By Train Daily trains leave Chamartín station in Madrid for Granada, and there are fairly straightforward connections with Barcelona and Valencia. There are also trains to Córdoba and Seville, although buses to those cities are faster and cheaper. The Granada train station is at the end of Avenida Anadaluces. City bus no. 11 shuttles between the station and several downtown stops. Call RENFE (tel. 958-27-12-72) for information about arrivals and departures.

By Bus The major bus company in the area is Alsina Gräells (tel. 956/25-13-58), with its own terminal at Camino de Ronda 97. It serves Granada and Seville, Córdoba, Málaga, and smaller Andalucian cities and towns. Bacoma (tel. 958/28-42-51) provides buses to and from such east coast cities as Valencia and Murcia; its buses arrive at and depart from the train station (Avenida Andaluces 10).

By Car A new highway between Granada and Seville was built in time for the 1992 Expo, so the driving time between the two cities is less than 3 hours. Route N-IV from Madrid to Bailén (a small crossroads town) has been substantially improved. From there, the route is numbered 323 or E902, leading through Jaen to Granada. Some sections through wide valleys can be covered rather quickly, while other segments over the mountains are slower. The trip takes 5 or 6 hours, depending on weather and traffic.

CÓRDOBA

The ancient capital of Moorish Spain is only 86 miles east of Seville, 102 miles northwest of Granada, and 248 miles south of Madrid. Most of the roads leading there have only two lanes, but they are acceptable in terms of maintenance and traffic. Attractions of touristic interest—the Cathedral/Mosque and the old Jewish Quarter—lie along the left, or northerly, bank of the Guadalquivir River, encircled by the modern city that emerged around the walls of the Moors and Christian kings. A bridge built on Roman foundations connects them to the still newer city on the south side.

Getting There

By Train   A splendid high-speed train called the AVE was completed in time for the 1992 Seville Expo. It cut the travel time between Madrid and Seville from more than 7 hours to 2¹/₂. Córdoba is one of the few stops on that route—about 45 minutes from Seville and about 1³/₄ hours from Madrid. Several other trains run daily to Córdoba from those cities and from Málaga, including the express *talgo* trains, but they are much slower. Córdoba's Estación Central (tel. 957/23-89-26), renovated and expanded to serve the AVE, is situated off the Avenida de América, west of the old city.

By Bus   Several private bus companies provide good to excellent service to and from cities and towns throughout Andalucía. A company frequently used by visitors is Alsina Gräells (tel. 957/23-64-74) at Avenida Medina Azahara 29. It provides frequent service to Granada and Seville, as well as other cities in the area.

By Car   National route N-IV from Madrid has been upgraded in recent years, reducing driving time to Córdoba to about 4 hours. Seville is only about 2 hours away via the secondary road 431, or 1¹/₂ hours by the improved E05.

SEVILLE

Ingratiating Seville, with an estimated population of 665,000, is the capital of the eight-province region of Andalucía, which stretches in a deep band all the way across the bottom of the country to Portugal. The city straddles the Guadalquivir, which is navigable all the way from the Mediterranean, more than 50 miles to the south. Most of the major sights are in that part of the city to the east of the river. With a few exceptions, they are within walking distance of each other. A metro system is under construction but is not yet functional. Expensive but romantic horsedrawn carriages are alternative means of transportation.

Getting There

By Plane   Expanded and upgraded San Pablo Airport (tel. 95/451-0677) is less than 8 miles from the city center. It receives nonstop flights from every major city in Spain and many more from European capitals. From North America, it is necessary to change planes at Madrid. Iberia Airlines (tel. 901/421-8800) has an office in Seville at Almirante Lobo 3. There is no bus or train service from the airport, but taxis aren't too expensive.

By Train   A new railbed was installed prior to Seville's 1992 Expo to carry the new high-speed AVE trains from Madrid. Based on French technology, they have reduced the travel time between the two cities from more than 7 hours to $2^1/2$. Several cheaper, slower trains make the run daily. Santa Justa Station is a modern terminal built to handle the AVE and is fully equal to its task.

By Bus   Private companies provide frequent service from Málaga, Granada, Cádiz, Córdoba, Jerez de la Frontera, and Madrid, as well as other cities of the region. Except for the AVE train between Madrid and Seville, buses are nearly always faster and cheaper than trains. Comforts and conveniences vary from one bus company to another, however.

By Car   Divided highways connect Seville with Jerez, Cádiz, Granada, and Málaga. The two principal routes from Madrid are not as direct as might be wished, one of them via Mérida, the other by way of Ciudad Real and Córdoba. They have four-lane segments for only part of the way, but they are well maintained and traffic generally isn't too heavy.

SALAMANCA

Only 60 miles from the walled city of Avila and 127 from Madrid, the medieval university town of Salamanca spreads along the north bank of the River Tormes. Its present population is around 160,000 residents, of whom about 15,000 are students. The heart of the city is enclosed by a U-shaped string of streets that roughly follows the ancient walled perimeter. Most of the neighborhoods within this district are easily visited on foot, with the arcaded Plaza Mayor at the approximate center. Two vehicular bridges and a pedestrian-only span constructed by the Romans connect the city with the highways south of the river.

Getting There

By Train   Madrid's Estación del Norte on Paseo del Rey 30 has trains to Salamanca three times a day from Monday through Saturday. The trip takes $3^1/2$ hours. There are no trains on Sunday. The Salamanca station is about a 10-minute taxi ride from the Plaza Mayor, on Avenida Estación Ferrocarril (Railway Station Avenue).

By Bus   Faster and cheaper than trains, at least from Madrid, buses from the Auto-Res station (tel. 91/551-7200 or 91/551-8404) at Plaza Conde de Casal 6 in Madrid reach Salamanca by nonstop express in $2^1/2$ hours or in 3 hours with some stops. There are departures every hour from early morning to late evening, every day. The station in Salamanca is at Avenida Filiberto Villalobos 73, about a 10-minute drive or 20-minute walk from the Plaza Mayor.

By Car   From Madrid, take the divided A-6 *autopista* as far as Villacastín, pick up N-110 to Avila (certainly worth a layover), then N-501 to Salamanca. The drive takes about 3 hours, not counting stops.

FAST FACTS   **Spain's Cities**

American Express   Travel service offices are located in Barcelona, at Carrer Roselló 257 (tel. 93/217-0070); Granada at Avenida de la Constitución 19 (tel. 958/27-63-12); Madrid, at Plaza de las Cortés 2 (tel. 91/322-5500); and Seville, at Teniente Coronel Seguí 6 (tel. 95/421-2923). Most are open from Monday through Friday 10am to 1:30pm and 5 to 8pm and Saturday from 10am to 1:30pm.

Area Codes   The telephone area code is 93 in Barcelona, 957 in Córdoba, 958 in Granada, 91 in Madrid, 923 in Salamanca, and 956 in Seville. Area codes are required when calling from outside the code. Note that all these area codes begin with "9," omit the "9" when calling Spain from outside the country.

Auto Rental   All the major U.S. car-rental firms are represented, with counters at the larger airports and offices in the cities. Advance arrangements before leaving for Spain are often cheaper than deals made on arrival. Call toll-free in the U.S. for rates:

Hertz (tel. 800/654-3131), **Avis** (tel. 800/831-2847), **National** (tel. 800/227-7368). National is known as **Europcar** in Spain. When shopping for the best rates, consider the U.S. discount firm, **Kenwel** (tel. 800/678-0678). Their cars are comparable to the big three but are less expensive. The major firm in Spain is **Atesa;** its Madrid office is at Calle Orense 83 (tel. 91/571-2145). In addition, most cities have smaller, local companies that can offer significant savings on comparable vehicles. Two that have proved to be reliable in the past are **Vanguard** and **Totcar,** both of which have offices in all of the cities covered in this book except Salamanca. The trade-off is that there are fewer options, such as rent-it-here-leave-it-there, and fewer possibilities for replacement and repair. To minimize risks, it's wise to accept only unlimited mileage deals and to make certain that collision coverage and taxes are included in the quoted price.

Business Hours   Most banks are open Monday through Friday from 9am to 2pm and 9am to 1pm on Saturday. A few reopen their currency exchange windows from 4 to 6pm. Offices are usually open Monday through Friday from 9am to 1 or 2pm and 5 to 7 or 8pm. Museums observe hours similar to those of stores and offices, except they are usually open on Sunday and closed Monday. Some museums are now staying open through the customary afternoon siesta period, as are branches of the two major department store chains, El Corte Inglés and Gallerías Preciados. Most stores continue, however, to observe the siesta, which means they are open Monday through Saturday from 9:30 or 10am to 1:30pm and 5 to 8pm. Some close on Saturday afternoon, and nearly all are closed Sunday. The rare exceptions to the Sunday closing are shops that cater to tourists.

Restaurants typically open at 1:30 until 4pm for lunch, then from 8:30 or 9 to 11:30pm or later. Bars, taverns, and cafeterías are usually open from early morning to 11pm or midnight, without a break, so it is always possible to get something to eat. Cocktail lounges and other "bars of the night," where little or no food is served, are usually open from 8pm until 3 or 4am. Discos and nightclubs may open as late as midnight and close at 4 or 5am. Cinemas in the larger cities have three shows a day, as a rule, typically at or around 4pm, 7pm, and 10pm.

Currency   The basic monetary unit is the peseta, abbreviated as "pta." Theoretically, 1 peseta is composed of 100 centavos, and there are still some 50-centavo pieces in circulation. But since the peseta is worth less than a U.S. penny, centavos are irrelevant. There are coins in the amount of 1, 5, 25, 50, 100, 200, and 500 pesetas, and bills in denominations of 500 (infrequent), 1,000, 5,000, and 10,000 pesetas. Older coins, minted during the Franco regime and bearing his likeness, are still in circulation and can be confused with newer coins, most of which carry the image of King Juan Carlos. Similar in size and appearance are the old 5 and new 200-peseta coins and especially the new 100- and 500-peseta coins. The most useful coin is the new 100; chunky and gold-colored, they are convenient to carry for tipping doormen, porters, ushers, and chambermaids.

Currency Exchange   Although it is useful to carry a few dollars in cash for emergencies and for expenses upon arrival back home, traveler's checks are not only safer to carry in the event of theft or loss but also command more favorable exchange rates. With the wide availability of automatic teller machines (ATMs) throughout Spain, not only in cities but also in towns and even small villages, travelers can gain access to their home checking and savings accounts through the Cirrus and Plus networks. Most machines offer directions in four to six languages, including English. A four-digit personal identification number (PIN) is required to operate the ATMs. The same machines also give cash advances against major credit cards. Cash withdrawals and advances are paid only in pesetas. These exchange rates are usually better than those given at exchange desks in banks and by hotels. One caveat: some North American banks charge hefty fees for using foreign ATMs; therefore, you should determine your bank's fees before departure. Free-standing exchange booths that advertise "no commission" are found in abundance in tourist areas of the larger cities. They are open for much longer hours than banks, but you should consider them for emergencies only, since they pay significantly lower rates in order to make their profits.

Driving Rules   Seat belts must be worn outside city limits, according to law, and directional signals must be used when one is changing lanes and passing other vehicles. Right turns cannot be made at red lights. In many cities, after one turns at a green light, there is an immediate second light, meant to permit pedestrians to cross. Children under 12 must ride in the rear seat unless belts specifically intended for them are installed in the front seat. Yield to vehicles entering an intersection from the right, except when in a traffic circle.

Police do not chase speeders. Instead, they use road blocks and radar. If you are pulled over, be prepared to show your driver's license, passport, and car-rental agreement or registration and insurance documents. Fines must be paid on the spot, in amounts that can exceed 5,000 pesetas. There is no guarantee, but some officers can be persuaded to add the fine to the car-rental agreement, which you can then pay with a credit card along with the cost of the rental. Highway police, usually of the Guardia Civil paramilitary force, rarely speak English.

Drugstores   *Farmacías* take turns staying open late. The *farmacías de guardia* are often listed in the daily newspapers and on the doors of pharmacies themselves. Hotel *conserjes* usually know the location of the nearest open drugstore, too.

Electricity   The Spanish electrical current is 220 volts, 50 cycles AC, and the standard plug has two *round* prongs. Since the North American current is 110–115 volts, 60 cycles, U.S. and Canadian visitors will need adaptors to use their appliances in Spain. If those appliances do not convert from 110 to 220 volts with the flip of a switch, as many hairdryers do, for example, you will need converters or transformers for those appliances. A further complication is that most U.S. appliances now have plugs with one prong with a splayed end for safety, and these don't fit in most available adaptors or in Spanish sockets. It would be a good idea to consult the manufacturers of any appliances to be used, especially of more expensive machines, such as laptop and notebook computers and printers.

Embassies   The **U.S. Embassy** in Madrid is at Calle Serrano 75 (tel. 91/577-4040). The **Canadian Embassy** is at Calle Nuñez de Balboa 35 (tel. 91/431-4300), and the **U.K. Embassy** is at Calle Fernando el Santo 16 (tel. 91/319-0200). Inquire by telephone about their hours before making the trip.

Emergencies   In the major cities, dial 091 or 092 for police (*policia*) assistance. In Barcelona, dial 080 for the fire brigade (*bombers*) and 329-7766 for an ambulance (*ambulància*). In Madrid, dial 232-3232 for the fire department (*cuerpo de bomberos*) and 252-3264 for an ambulance (*ambulància*). In Seville, dial 091 for fire and 433-0993 for an ambulance.

There are several useful words in an emergency, all of them easy to remember and pronounce: *¡Socorro!* (Help!) *¡Policia! ¡Accidente! ¡Ambulància! ¡Doctor!*

Fax Services   Most of the better hotels have fax machines available to guests. Central post offices and telephone offices usually have fax services, too, as do the many copy shops. Faxes (the word is the same in Spanish) can be received only in hotels with machines, not at the other types of agencies. In addition, keep in mind that room reservations made by fax provide written confirmation in the event of confusion upon arrival.

Information   Barcelona has several tourist information offices: at the airport and railroad stations and downtown at Gran Via de les Cortes Catalanes 658 (tel. 93/301-7443). They are open Monday to Friday from 9am to 7pm, Saturday until 2pm.

Madrid has tourist offices at the airport and the Chamartín train station. The one on the Plaza España at Princesa 1 (tel. 91/541-2325) is open Monday through Friday from 9am to 7pm, Saturday from 9:30am to 1:30pm.

Seville's main tourist office is near the Cathedral at Avenida 21B (tel. 95/422-1404), and there is a branch at the airport. Córdoba has a modest information office on Plaza de Judá Levi (tel. 957/47-20-00). Granada's tourist office is at Plaza Mariana Pineda 10 (tel. 958/22-66-88), and in Salamanca, there is a tourist office at Gran Vía 41 (tel. 923/26-85-71).

Liquor Laws   Although 16 is the legal drinking age, this law is enforced with considerable flexibility. Bottles of beer, wine, brandy, and other spirits are sold at corner convenience stores, *charcuterías,* and at markets during regular business hours. These are sold by the glass during all open hours of bars, taverns, *cafeterías,* and eating establishments.

Lost Property   In most cases, it is best to ask the hotel *conserje* to assist you, since lost-and-found offices are located at airports, town halls, metro systems, police stations, and other locations, and fluency in Spanish is essential. If that isn't possible, try the nearest police station or the main office of the store or transportation facility where you may have lost the item.

Mail   Post offices (*correos*) are normally open Monday through Friday from 8 or 9am to 1am and 5 to 7pm and Saturday 9am to 1pm. The main post offices in the larger cities often stay open through the siesta and keep certain windows open as late as midnight. They will keep mail addressed to individuals at *Lista de Correos,* followed by the zip code, the name of the town, and the province. The surname of the addressee should be underlined, since Spaniards typically bear both their maternal and paternal names and letters could be filed under the wrong name. A passport is required to pick up mail at a *lista de correos.*

Alternatively, mail will be kept for a month at American Express offices for customers who hold the Amex charge card or who possess Amex travelers checks.

Newspapers and Magazines   The *International Herald Tribune* is widely circulated, at least in the larger cities and major resorts. Editions available in Spain are published in France and so are usually current. *USA Today* is often available, but is more likely to be a day or two late. *The Wall Street Journal* is also seen but less regularly. British readers can often find copies of *The Times, The Guardian, The Daily Telegraph,* and *The Independent.* A weekly, *The European,* is of peripheral interest. *Time, Newsweek,* and, less often, *U.S. News & World Report* are usually available at the same outlets. Many U.S. and British magazines have siblings in Spanish, occasionally next to copies of the English-language originals. In Barcelona and Madrid, a weekly magazine called *Guía del Ocio* ("Leisure Guide") lists current attractions, art exhibits, concerts and films, as well as capsule descriptions of restaurants, bars, and nightclubs. It's in Spanish but not difficult to decipher. Prominent national newspapers include the left-of-center *El Mundo* and *El País,* as well as the conservative *ABC.* Catalunya's most important publication is *La Vanguardia.*

Police   In emergencies, call 091. If that doesn't work (and it may not in smaller towns or remote location), dial the operator and ask to be connected with the nearest police station.

Restrooms   Public toilets are few, and those found in metro stations and pedestrian underpasses are invariably grim and potentially unsafe. Fortunately, almost every block has a bar or two, and most of them have adequate facilities. Better still, duck into the lobby of a larger, better-class hotel and try to look like a paying guest while seeking out a restroom. Museums are another possibility, but an entrance fee must be paid.

Safety   Democracy has brought prosperity, increased the size of the middle class, and dismantled the former police state. Unfortunately, it has also widened the gap between rich and poor and allowed the growth of the traffic in illegal drugs. All this, combined with an unemployment rate exceeding 25% in some regions, has stimulated a substantial rise in street crime. Tourists have a tendency to feel immune from grifters and muggers, when they are actually prime targets. Although street crime is seldom as violent as in the United States, Americans should follow the same precautions they observe in cities back home.

There are some special twists to crime in Spain that tourists need to be aware of. In some cities, hoodlums leap from a hiding place to attack cars stopped at traffic lights, breaking windows and grabbing anything within reach. Jewelry- and purse-snatching are epidemic, either on foot or from the back of motorcycles. Pickpockets work in teams, one distracting the mark by spilling something on a sleeve or feinting a grab at a visible possession while an associate plucks a wallet, empties a purse, or grabs a camera. The obvious precautions a visitor could take are too often ignored. A short list would include: using hotel safes, leaving expensive or flashy jewelry at home, wearing a money belt or pouch, avoiding unlighted streets and plazas, taking taxis at night door-to-door, and leaving nothing of value in a car, including the trunk.

Taxes   The value-added tax on products and services is called an "IVA" in Spain. For some time, the IVA was variable, ranging from as little as 6% to as high as 15% at four- and five-star hotels and luxury restaurants. In January 1995, the IVA was lowered to a uniform 7%, to the relief of the hospitality industry and its customers. There is no airport departure tax.

Telephone   There are few instruments more intimidating than the telephone in a foreign country where the caller doesn't speak the language. Spain tries to make it easier for its visitors. Most public telephone booths on the streets of the larger cities have instructions written in English. In some, it is possible to press a button and receive succinct, step-by-step directions in English on a small screen above the keypad. Of course, if the person at the other end answers with the usual abrupt "*¡Digáme!*" ("Talk to me!"), panic can bubble up instantly. For the non-Spanish-speaking, the only course is to ask immediately, "*¿Habla usted inglés?*" or just "Do you speak English?"

The ringing signal is a slow, repeating tone, while the busy signal is shorter and more rapid. All area codes in Spain start with "9" and are followed by the code of the province. Omit the "9" if calling from outside Spain. To call the United States or Canada from Spain, dial "07," wait for the higher pitched international tone, then "1," the area code, and the number. To call the United Kingdom, follow the same sequence except dial "44" before the area code.

Some public phones accept the prepaid calling card known as a *tarjeta telefónica,* which is available in denominations of 1,000 and 2,000 pesetas. They can be purchased at *estancos* (tobacconists), post offices, and central telephone offices. These special phones also accept some credit cards. The three major U.S. long-distance companies provide access numbers to their customers that not only substantially reduce charges but also connect the caller immediately with an English-speaking operator. The numbers are: AT&T (tel. 900/99-0011); MCI (tel. 900/99-0014); and Sprint (tel. 900/99-0013). Most operators in the larger hotels speak enough English to be helpful, but there are often stunning surcharges on long-distance calls made from hotels.

Television   Satellite technology use is growing, as opposed to cable systems. Most of the better hotels have TV channels in languages other than Spanish or Catalan, usually French, German, Italian, and English. The 24-hour news channel CNN is widely available, as is its rather parochial competitor, England's Sky News. Others that you might encounter are the NBC Super Channel, with 24 hours of news and talk; Eurosport, a sports channel; and a European version of MTV. Entertainment channels in English have yet to make a dent, but by channel-surfing you may find an English-language movie with Spanish subtitles.

Time   All of Spain is in a single time zone, six hours ahead of Eastern Standard Time and one hour ahead of the United Kingdom. Between April and October, Spain jumps ahead an extra hour for Daylight Saving Time. That switch is made slightly ahead of the United States in both spring and fall.

Tipping   Restaurants add a service charge, but leaving an additional 5%–10% is customary. Bellhops usually get 100 pesetas per bag, a little more if the luggage is especially heavy or must be carried a long way. It is customary to leave about 100 pesetas per night for chambermaids. Tip cab drivers, bartenders, barbers, and hairdressers about 10% of the bill. Ushers at bullrings and theaters should be tipped a small amount, no more than 100 pesetas. The man who pumps gas at a service station usually gets a similar amount. Tour guides, often forgotten, should be given 200 to 400 pesetas, depending upon the length of the tour and your evaluation of the guide's competence. Nevertheless, always remember that a tip is for satisfactory service, and if you do not receive it, you should reduce the tip or withhold it altogether.

Water   Except where there are specific cautions, as on trains, water is potable almost everywhere. It rarely tastes very good, however, so people usually order mineral water (*agua*) with meals, either still (*sin gas*) or spritzed (*con gas*). Bottled water can be purchased in food stores and markets.

RECOMMENDED READING

Nonfiction   Spain has provoked the muse in foreign artists, writers, and social critics since the Roman legions first stepped ashore. They have provided a wealth of materials from which to gain insights into Spaniards and their densely layered culture. The following suggestions merely hint at what is available.

The Australian Robert Hughes, the erudite, acerbic art critic for *Time* magazine, wrote *Barcelona* in anticipation of the 1992 Olympics. He combines scholarship and passion in his examination of Spain's second city. An Englishman, the travel writer H. V. Morton, set down his impressions in *A Stranger in Spain* in 1955. It is still a good guide for present-day Spain, and a paperback version was issued in 1986. Travel writer extraordinaire Jan Morris wrote a series of essays on the Spanish character to accompany the photographs of a 1964 coffee-table book called *Spain.* This was one of those rare occasions when the companion text outshone the pictures, and so the book, sans photos, was subsequently revised and reissued in 1979 and again a decade later. Another useful exploration of soul rather than stone is *The Spanish Temper* by V. S. Pritchett, the British critic and novelist. Although it was last published in 1955, local libraries may have copies.

The trauma of Spain's 1936–39 Civil War and its coldly calculated function as a Fascist training ground for World War II has been examined relentlessly by scholars and ideologues in the intervening decades. The clear front-runner for objectivity and comprehensiveness is *The Spanish Civil War* by British historian Hugh Thomas. First published in 1961, it has been revised and enlarged since, most recently in 1977. *Blood of Spain* (1979) is a thick compilation of oral recollections of the war by participants and victims on both sides, by Ronald Fraser. Other Englishmen have provided more personal insights into the conflict. Novelist and journalist George Orwell joined one of the militias fighting for the Loyalist cause during the war and wrote *Homage to Catalonia* (1952) while on the scene. Memoirist Laurie Lee has penned compelling accounts in two slim volumes. *As I Walked Out One Midsummer Morning* limns his sojourn across the peninsula in the months before the outbreak of hostilities, while *A Moment of War* tells of his brief period of service, culminating at the bloody Teruel front. *Federico Garcia Lorca: A Life* (1989) tells of an early victim of that war—the Spanish poet and playwright; more of his works have been translated into other languages than those of any other Spanish artist. The author is Ian Gibson, whose knowledge of Garcia Lorca is so deep that he writes more often in Spanish than in English.

The British have a known affinity for Spain, or at least a pronounced curiosity about the country that is geographically so near yet so different from their own. This began with the several conflicts in which they were either allied or opposed to the Spanish kings and continued with such pioneering travel writers as Richard Ford, who wrote about his Iberian journeys, often with clucks of dismay, in *Gatherings from Spain* (1846) and *Handbook for Travellers in Spain* (1845). Each of these has been reprinted in recent years.

Fewer American writers have been drawn to Spain, but those who have been caught up in the passion of its people fill the gaps. The most celebrated American aficionado is certainly Ernest Hemingway. His frequent excursions and stays there—for bullfights, battles, and fishing—are detailed in Carlos Baker's *Ernest Hemingway: A Life Story,* first published in 1968 and still available in paperback. James A. Michener put his prodigious storytelling skills to use in his equally thick tome *Iberia.* Somewhat dated now, it nevertheless retains many insights into Spanish culture and society. It was published the same year as the Hemingway biography and is also still in print. Less well known is the fact that Washington Irving, the creator of Rip Van Winkle, was also a diplomat. While serving as an attaché at the U.S. Embassy in Madrid from 1826 to 1832, he wrote a biography of Columbus, and during long stays in Seville and Granada assembled his *Tales of the Alhambra.*

The origins of Spain reach back into prehistory, exemplified by the luminous cave paintings at Altamira in the northwest. If history is written by the victors, however, it might seem that Spain has been a Catholic nation since the dawn of Christianity, ruled by monarchs called Isabel and Fernando and Felipe. But once, before the advent of the Inquisition, there were centuries of rule by Romans proconsuls and Arab caliphs, and Jews such as the philosopher Maimonides lived among them. Two recent books focus on these other peoples and cultures, reflecting democratic Spain's fresh willingness to examine its past. The Sephardic Jewish experience is receiving renewed attention, as in *The Jews of Spain* (1992) by Jane S. Gerber, a professor of Jewish history at the City University of New York. *Moorish Spain* (1992), by Richard Fletcher, a British historian whose special interest is Spain, outlines the achievements and struggles of the Arab hegemony, which lasted from 711 to 1492.

The variegated architecture of Spain's many regions and epochs keeps heads swiveling on even the shortest visits. A standard, comprehensive work on the subject is *History of Spanish Architecture* by Bernard Bevan. An expanded edition is in preparation now. Much of the visual interest of rural villages is provided by vernacular structures, architecture without architects created by locals who use whatever materials are at hand to deal with the terrain and climate in which they find themselves. A fascinating study of the results of centuries of such improvisation is *Iberian Villages: Portugal & Spain* (1981) by Norman F. Carver, Jr., an architect and photographer who also wrote the text for this picture book. Straightforward discussions of architectural styles and trends are presented in sections of the *Blue Guide: Spain* by Ian Robertson and the *Michelin Tourist Guide: Spain.*

Fiction   No American writer is more closely associated with Spain than Hemingway, although he also lived and worked in many other places. *The Sun Also Rises,* his second published novel, follows British and American expatriates who travel from Paris to Pamplona to participate in the San Fermín festival. It made that city's running of the bulls a world-famous event, a fact duly noted by a bust of Hemingway that stands in a place of honor near the bullring. A final scene in the book has his protagonists dining at the atmospheric Meson Botín, Madrid's oldest restaurant. Later he penned *For Whom the Bell Tolls,* about an American demolitions expert who aids a band of guerrillas on the Loyalist side, and *Death in the Afternoon,* a nonfiction work that analyzes the spectacle of bullfighting.

No homegrown literary achievement surpasses Miguel de Cervantes Saavedra's satirical masterwork, *Don Quijote.* The essentials of the plot are well known, owing to the popularity of the musical version, *Man of La Mancha,* and the subsequent film. What is less appreciated, perhaps, is the book's profound influence upon the development of the novel form. It was completed in 1615, after all, when reading was still a pleasure largely limited to the privileged classes. A frequently cited translation of *Don Quijote* is the one by Samuel Putnam (1949). While no Spanish novelist has since eclipsed the bright light radiated by Cervantes, Camilo José Cela won a Nobel Prize in Literature in 1989. His work is noted for its grotesque, nightmarish naturalism and for breaking long-standing Spanish taboos about depictions of sexuality. His first novel, *The Family of Pascual Duarte* (1942); and one of the most recent, *Mazurka for Two Dead Men,* are highly regarded and available in English translations. The predilection of Spanish novelists to engage in literary experiment and surrealism has tended to discourage translations into English. A few who have been successful in this regard, however, include: Miguel Delibes, with *Five Hours with Mario* and *The Prince Dethroned;* Juan Benet, with *You'll Never Get Anywhere* and *A Meditation;* and Francisco Ayala, with *The Lamb's Head* and *Usurpers.*

INDEX

BARCELONA

MADRID

GRANADA (ALHAMBRA)

CÓRDOBA

SEVILLE

SALAMANCA

Now Save Money on All Your Travels by Joining

Frommer's
TRAVEL BOOK CLUB

The Advantages of Membership:

1. Your choice of any **TWO FREE BOOKS.**

2. Your own subscription to the **TRIPS & TRAVEL** quarterly newsletter, where you'll discover the best buys in travel, the hottest vacation spots, the latest travel trends, world-class events and festivals, and much more.

3. A **30% DISCOUNT** on any additional books you order through the club.

4. **DOMESTIC TRIP-ROUTING KITS** (available for a small additional fee). We'll send you a detailed map highlighting the most direct or scenic route to your destination, anywhere in North America.

Here's all you have to do to join:

Send in your annual membership fee of $25.00 ($35.00 Canada/Foreign) with your name, address, and selections on the form below. Or call 815/734-1104 to use your credit card.

Send all orders to:

FROMMER'S TRAVEL BOOK CLUB
P.O. Box 473 • Mt. Morris, IL 61054-0473 • ☎ 815/734-1104

YES! I want to take advantage of this opportunity to join Frommer's Travel Book Club.

[ ] My check for $25.00 ($35.00 for Canadian or foreign orders) is enclosed.
   All orders must be prepaid in U.S. funds only. Please make checks payable to Frommer's Travel Book Club.

[ ] Please charge my credit card: [ ] Visa or [ ] Mastercard

   Credit card number: _____

   Expiration date: ___ / ___ / ___

   Signature: _____

   Or call 815/734-1104 to use your credit card by phone.

Name: _____

Address: _____

City: _____ State: _____ Zip code: _____

Phone number (in case we have a question regarding your order): _____

Please indicate your choices for TWO FREE books (*see following pages*):

   Book 1 - Code: _____ Title: _____

   Book 2 - Code: _____ Title: _____

For information on ordering additional titles, see your first issue of the *Trips & Travel* newsletter.

Allow 4–6 weeks for delivery for all items. Prices of books, membership fee, and publication dates are subject to change without notice. All orders are subject to acceptance and availability.

The following Frommer's guides are available from your favorite
bookstore, or you can use the order form on the preceding page
to request them as part of your membership in
Frommer's Travel Book Club.

FROMMER'S COMPLETE TRAVEL GUIDES

*(Comprehensive guides to sightseeing, dining and accommodations,
with selections in all price ranges—from deluxe to budget)*

FROMMER'S $-A-DAY GUIDES

(Dream Vacations at Down-to-Earth Prices)

FROMMER'S COMPLETE CITY GUIDES

(Comprehensive guides to sightseeing, dining, and accommodations in all price ranges)

Amsterdam, 8th Ed.	S176	Miami '95-'96	S149
Athens, 10th Ed.	S174	Minneapolis/St. Paul, 4th Ed.	S159
Atlanta & the Summer Olympic		Montréal/Québec City '95	S166
Games '96 (avail. 11/95)	S181	Nashville/Memphis, 1st Ed.	S141
Atlantic City/Cape May,		New Orleans '96 (avail. 10/95)	S182
5th Ed.	S130	New York City '96 (avail. 11/95)	S183
Bangkok, 2nd Ed.	S147	Paris '96 (avail. 9/95)	S180
Barcelona '93-'94	S115	Philadelphia, 8th Ed.	S167
Berlin, 3rd Ed.	S162	Prague, 1st Ed.	S143
Boston '95	S160	Rome, 10th Ed.	S168
Budapest, 1st Ed.	S139	St. Louis/Kansas City, 2nd Ed.	S127
Chicago '95	S169	San Antonio/Austin, 1st Ed.	S177
Denver/Boulder/		San Diego '95	S158
Colorado Springs, 3rd Ed.	S154	San Francisco '96 (avail. 10/95)	S184
Disney World/Orlando '96		Santa Fe/Taos/	
(avail. 9/95)	S178	Albuquerque '95	S172
Dublin, 2nd Ed.	S157	Seattle/Portland '94-'95	S137
Hong Kong '94-'95	S140	Sydney, 4th Ed.	S171
Las Vegas '95	S163	Tampa/St. Petersburg, 3rd Ed.	S146
London '96 (avail. 9/95)	S179	Tokyo '94-'95	S144
Los Angeles '95	S164	Toronto, 3rd Ed.	S173
Madrid/Costa del Sol, 2nd Ed.	S165	Vancouver/Victoria '94-'95	S142
Mexico City, 1st Ed.	S175	Washington, D.C. '95	S153

FROMMER'S FAMILY GUIDES

(Guides to family-friendly hotels, restaurants, activities, and attractions)

California with Kids	F105	San Francisco with Kids	F104
Los Angeles with Kids	F103	Washington, D.C. with Kids	F102
New York City with Kids	F101		

FROMMER'S WALKING TOURS

(Memorable strolls through colorful and historic neighborhoods, accompanied by detailed directions and maps)

Berlin	W100	San Francisco, 2nd Ed.	W115
Chicago	W107	Spain's Favorite Cities	
England's Favorite Cities	W108	(avail. 9/95)	W116
London, 2nd Ed.	W111	Tokyo	W109
Montréal/Québec City	W106	Venice	W110
New York, 2nd Ed.	W113	Washington, D.C., 2nd Ed.	W114
Paris, 2nd Ed.	W112		

FROMMER'S AMERICA ON WHEELS

(Guides for travelers who are exploring the U.S.A. by car, featuring a brand-new rating system for accommodations and full-color road maps)

Arizona/New Mexico	A100	Florida	A102
California/Nevada	A101	Mid-Atlantic	A103

FROMMER'S SPECIAL-INTEREST TITLES

Arthur Frommer's Branson!	P107	Frommer's Where to	
Arthur Frommer's New World		Stay U.S.A., 11th Ed.	P102
of Travel (avail. 11/95)	P112	National Park Guide, 29th Ed.	P106
Frommer's Caribbean		USA Today Golf	
Hideaways (avail. 9/95)	P110	Tournament Guide	P113
Frommer's America's 100		USA Today Minor League	
Best-Loved State Parks	P109	Baseball Book	P111

FROMMER'S BEST BEACH VACATIONS

(The top places to sun, stroll, shop, stay, play, party, and swim—with each beach rated for beauty, swimming, sand, and amenities)

California (avail. 10/95)	G100	Hawaii (avail. 10/95)	G102
Florida (avail. 10/95)	G101		

FROMMER'S BED & BREAKFAST GUIDES

(Selective guides with four-color photos and full descriptions of the best inns in each region)

California	B100	Hawaii	B105
Caribbean	B101	Pacific Northwest	B106
East Coast	B102	Rockies	B107
Eastern United States	B103	Southwest	B108
Great American Cities	B104		

FROMMER'S IRREVERENT GUIDES

(Wickedly honest guides for sophisticated travelers and those who want to be)

Chicago (avail. 11/95)	I100	New Orleans (avail. 11/95)	I103
London (avail. 11/95)	I101	San Francisco (avail. 11/95)	I104
Manhattan (avail. 11/95)	I102	Virgin Islands (avail. 11/95)	I105

FROMMER'S DRIVING TOURS

(Four-color photos and detailed maps outlining spectacular scenic driving routes)

Australia	Y100	Italy	Y108
Austria	Y101	Mexico	Y109
Britain	Y102	Scandinavia	Y110
Canada	Y103	Scotland	Y111
Florida	Y104	Spain	Y112
France	Y105	Switzerland	Y113
Germany	Y106	U.S.A.	Y114
Ireland	Y107		

FROMMER'S BORN TO SHOP

(The ultimate travel guides for discriminating shoppers—from cut-rate to couture)

Hong Kong (avail. 11/95)	Z100	London (avail. 11/95)	Z101